Contents

Acknowledgements

No book gets written without the support of others. There are so many who have made their contributions, big and small, intentionally and unknowingly, I can't name them all. I can acknowledge the ones at the forefront, without whose support this book would never have been completed.

A special acknowledgement goes to Chuck for being my "adoring editor", making me breakfast every morning, and beautiful roses every week. You really are a master communicator!

My boys- Alex and Carter. Everyday, you show me how much I've learned and how far I have to go. You are my greatest gift to the world.

The staff at Corporate Vision for your unwavering efforts, flexibility, good humor, and honest communication.

Stewart Emery who was the catalyst to a life of authentic expression.

To my clients. I am privileged to be included in your dreams and to be allowed to play a part in your accomplishments.

To my Goal Friends and Coach2 buddies for your inspiration, innovation, laughs, and for putting my feet to the fire!

All my friends at The Strategic Coach, starting with Dan Sullivan and Babs Smith. I love you guys and appreciate constantly being reminded of my unique ability and being given an opportunity to grow.

Casey & Rod for giving me a stage!

For so many friends who have ongoingly expressed their belief in me - Colleen, Debra, Julian, Gord, David, Doug to name a few.

To my very large, boisterous, funny, playful family who continually provide me with great material. Everyone should be so lucky to be surrounded by such amazing people.

I am very fortunate to be well loved and supported by family, friends, clients and colleagues. I do not take this blessing lightly, but treasure it as the gift it is. This book is a way for me to share all the gifts given to me so generously. Thank you to all those who have touched my life and made it so rich.

Author's Forward

After completing my MBA and spending several years working in marketing and sales, something was missing for me. Then, in the early 80's, I was introduced to the personal growth work of Stewart Emery and Carole Augustus at Actualizations in San Francisco. As a result I found my path. I saw a possibility for communication that would transcended the usual hype and hyperbole evident in most business interactions through that experience. I envisioned communication that would touch people more deeply than the norm, making it possible to enjoy the satisfaction of being our fully expressed, authentic selves. This has since become my life's passion and purpose- coaching individuals and organizations to be authentic and connected in their communication.

Over the past 25 years, I've learned a lot, yet I feel like I'm still in school, with plenty more to learn. I have avidly sought out experts in a variety of fields who I thought could shed light on how to connect better. I've had insights from unexpected places, like quantum physics and modern brain research. It has all contributed to the deepening of my own understanding of how we can make the most of our interactions with one another in a manner that is supportive and non-manipulative.

My coaching is based on the lessons I've learned from personal experience and the amazing people who have been my teachers. My coaching is also based on the lessons I'm still figuring out, where I'm struggling, and the mistakes I've made. Everyday, I learn something new. This book shares some of what I've learned so far. My intention is that after reading this book, you will have an expanded experience of yourself as a communicator and person, confident in the knowledge that you have a practical path to follow to the success and fulfillment you desire.

With great appreciation, I send my best wishes.

Teresa Easler
Toronto
June 2005

Introduction

Many of the people I coach say they feel confident and comfortable when they are presenting in a one on one situation, but put them in front of a group and the butterflies begin. They say they would like to feel the same kind of ease and get the same level results in both situations. The truth is, all presentations are really just conversations. What's different is how many people are in on the conversation and how many are verbal participants. When speakers see their presentations in this way, the anxiety they experience in front of groups is released. When we are having a conversation, we're just people, being with other folks.

As speakers, we normally think of communication as a means of transferring information, but it is much more than that. It's more than talking. It's more than listening too. It's about hearing. It's about the interaction of souls, sharing ideas, thoughts, convictions and passions. This book is about a specific type of communication, giving a speech or presentation. While focused on that particular format, the suggestions made can be applied to all types of communication, in any situation.

There are two keys to being a great speaker. First is the mastery of the knowledge and skills that make memorable presentations. I call this the "doing" part of communicating. Second and most important is who you are "being" when you communicate. It is important to remember, audiences tend to be more forgiving of speakers whose skills are not that polished if who they are "being" is authentic. There is no better way to establish a relationship of trust with an audience.

This first became apparent to me years ago when I was a poor university student, paying my way through school working as a waitress and tending bar in a resort town in Colorado. Every Friday and Saturday night, the restaurant where I worked had live music. There were two guitarists who performed regularly. Each played similar material, but with distinctively different styles. The first was one of the most technically proficient musicians I had ever heard. He played like Segovia, able to execute complicated chord combinations with the precision of a surgeon. The second guitarist, Ted, was a highly skilled musician, not at the same level as the first, but he played with abandon, heart and pure joy. Consistently, Ted drew a larger audience as a result of his sheer energy and passion.

The first guitarist was focused only on the "doing", while Ted exemplified the powerful combination of "doing" and "being." It's no coincidence that I remember Ted's name to this day, and the first musician's name faded from memory years ago.

As people and members of an audience, we have difficulty relating to speakers who offer lots of polish and oratorical technique, but very little humanity. It feels like they're just too "slick" or in some cases, outright "sleazy", not deserving of our trust. On some occasions we are consciously aware of what we are feeling, other times it subtly colors our experience. We lose interest. We don't remember much of what the speaker had to say. They just don't connect with the audience.

Caution: This is not an excuse for failing to develop solid communication skills and techniques. If you really want to be an effective speaker, it's the powerful combination of "doing" and "being" that leads to confidence, self-satisfaction, and stellar results.

I will get into both of these aspects of great communication. I'll cover "doing" through two templates. The first supports strategic thinking in advance of creating a presentation. The second template provides an easy to use framework for designing memorable presentations.

But first, I'll look at the three keys to the "being" aspect of effective communication, Authenticity, Creativity, and Connection. Each is closely interrelated so the lines between them can blur. Together, they are the foundation of powerful presentations that inspire and motivate an audience to take action.

Part One

BEING

CHAPTER 1

MORE THAN MECHANICS

When Chuck and I first created Bravo Presentation Coaching in 1996, we incorporated our belief that the best presentations went beyond just learning the mechanics of good speeches. Authenticity was a thread in all the most motivating, memorable speeches. As I continued to coach individuals and organizations on how to create and deliver presentations that get results, I saw two other themes emerge consistently: creativity and connection. As I observed great communicators, the people I coached and even myself speaking, I noticed that simultaneously being at ease with oneself to have all the attention on the audience while being open to spontaneous ideas separated the best from the

adequate. Authenticity, Connection, and Creativity are the foundation to the "Being" of great communication. Each of these plays a significant role in bridging the gulf between speaker and audience. The combination leads to the experiences all speakers want: the joy of knowing you hit one out of the park, confidence from capturing and holding the attention and imagination of a roomful of strangers, the gift of making a difference with others. Each of these has some characteristics in common, so the lines between them are not hard and fast. Think of them as the base of all your communication, strengthening each other and all that is built upon this foundation.

CHAPTER 2

AUTHENTICITY

What lies before us and what lies behind us are
small matters compared to what lies within us.
And when we bring what is within out
into the world, miracles happen.

Henry David Thoreau

We All Start Out As 360⁰ People

We all start out as 360^0 people. As infants we don't restrict ourselves.
When we want something, we let people know. When we don't like
something, we let people know. When we enjoy something, we let
people know. We are fully expressed, without inhibitions. Then we
get feedback from the outside world. Parents, family and visitors
start letting us know when our behavior is acceptable and when it is
not. Over time we respond by limiting how we express ourselves.
We want approval, so we adjust who we are being to fit what others
deem is proper. We begin sectioning off parts of ourselves. Then it's
off to school and we find out that the red high top sneakers we love
just aren't cool. So, we opt for the kind the other kids wear, even
though we don't like them as much. Then we become teenagers and
discover all the things the opposite sex likes or dislikes and we

respond accordingly by sealing off those parts of ourselves that may get a negative reaction. And then we enter the working world with its "rules" about what will and what will not help us get ahead. By the time we're in our 20's or 30's, we're no longer 360° people, but much more limited versions of our former selves. After a lifetime of others telling us what they expect and who they want us to be, we fall into a habit of being a lesser version of ourselves. The real sadness is that we believe this lesser version of ourselves is authentic. If we are told something often enough, we believe it. When we come to the realization that we are not being ourselves, it can be difficult to break through, because we have been being someone else for so long. Authenticity is the returning to self, returning to our innocence.

My cousin Deb's husband, Fred, is an interesting character in anyone's book. He's an ex-biker turned shaman who councils prison inmates on substance abuse. He's also one of the most authentic people I've ever met. He hasn't always been though. Much of his authenticity he attributes to his studies to become a shaman. When I asked him what he got out of his spiritual pursuits, he said it wasn't so much what he got as it was about what he got rid of. That's what it takes, getting rid of the things that suppress and distort who we really are. It's having the courage to shed the mantles we've added as protective armor, shielding ourselves from anticipated hurt or rejection.

I'm Not Enough

How that translates in a presentation is you feel the need to take on another persona in front of an audience. As human beings, quite often we do not bring our true self to our speaking for fear of rejection, of not being enough, of not being liked. After all, if we are our "real" self and the audience doesn't respond favorably, it feels very much like a personal rejection. So you put on your 'speaker's' persona. If the reaction is lukewarm or negative, it doesn't feel as personal. It's the mask they're rejecting, not the real you. As a result of this ill conceived idea that by not being yourself in your communication you are protecting yourself, you actually prevent the deep connection with your audience that occurs when you are being your authentic self. The audience can't be in relationship with the role you play. Relationship is only available with the authentic you. And connection is all about creating a relationship with the audience.

> "Let the world know
> you as you are,
> not as you think
> you should be,
> because sooner or later,
> if you are posing,
> you will forget the pose,
> and then where
> are you?"
>
> —Fanny Brice

CHAPTER 3

How Did We Get Into This Mess And How Do We Get Out?

Unconscious Of How We Feel

For the most part, we as human beings are unconscious of who we are being and operate on auto pilot, falling into the habit of being a whittled down version of who we really are. It becomes a habit. We loose touch with what's real for us, how we truly feel about our topic. And when we communicate, we tend to play a role that feels safe, rather than speak honestly. If this sounds like you, what is called for is to 'be present' to what is really going on for you and communicate it.

It's normal in this day and age to be focused externally. We all have busy lives with lots of concerns; delivering on deadlines, paying bills, picking up the kids from school, convincing someone to say yes to our products or services, motivating colleagues, staff and co-workers to take our lead.

Focusing externally robs you of being conscious of who you really are and how you really feel, of tapping into your authentic self. When you live like this, your communication comes out as rote, automatic, and you become disconnected from the people with whom you want or need to communicate. Most importantly, you are disconnected from yourself.

Invasion Of The Body Snatchers

This is one of the most dangerous traps for frequent and professional speakers. Many have their talk down pat; the gestures are perfect, the same way at the same time, every time. No stumbles, yet something is missing, a connection with how they truly feel about their subject. When most professional speakers start out, they have something important to say, a contribution they want to make, a powerful experience they want to share along with the lessons they've learned. Over time, some become disconnected from their message and the passion they once felt for it. The words come from memory. They become zombies or experience Invasion of the Body Snatchers. The body shows up, but there's no one home.

Discovering The Authentic Self

The first step in being a powerful communicator is being conscious of your authentic self, the one beneath the rented face you see in the mirror everyday. Having coached and spoken to hundreds of people about being an authentic speaker, a frequent question that comes up is, "How do I know who the authentic me is?" A good question and one with no fast answer, at least none that I've found for myself. This is one of the reasons mastering the 'being' aspect of communication is usually

> "Each of us is meant
> to have a character
> all our own,
> to be what no other
> can exactly be,
> and do what no
> other can exactly do."
>
> —William Ellery Channing

more difficult than the 'doing'. Finding your way back to your authentic self can be a life long process, but one rich in rewards.

I discovered an exercise in the book "The Energy of Money" by Dr. Maria Nemeth that helps in the process of uncovering the authentic self. In the exercise, you identify the people you admire, living or dead, historical, famous, relatives, co-workers and friends. Then, you list the qualities, characteristics or traits they exhibit that you admire. What this exercise reveals is that those things we resonate with in others, we ourselves possess. If we did not have these traits, we would not have the receptors to recognize them in others.

When I mentioned this exercise to a friend, he thought the word "admire" came from the root "to mirror". With a little research, I discovered that both "admire" and "mirror "do share the same Latin root, mirari, which means "to wonder at". The connection between the words admire and mirror is interesting, because the traits we see in others, that we 'wonder at', are the very same traits we posses and mirror back.

So often we focus more on the things we don't like about ourselves rather than our positive attributes. We have all heard that the things that drive us nuts in someone else are the very things we'd like to change in ourselves. How about the things we admire in others? These are the things I believe put us in touch with our authentic selves, the self we'd like to spend more time being in our lives. I found as I asked different people who they admire and why, they revealed more of their authentic selves. As I did the exercise for myself, I appreciated myself more. I felt more connected to what some would call my higher self, the real me.

I use my children as my guinea pigs to test ideas on how to coach people to be better communicators and better understand themselves. When I asked my boys who they admired, I was surprised at who they chose and who didn't make the list! For Carter, my youngest son, Julius Caesar was at the top of his hit parade. That may have been influenced by his recent studies at school, but I considered it a valid choice. He chose Caesar because he accomplished so much even though many people disagreed with him. Most of the other people who made his list got there because of their sense of humor and creative talent. When I asked if he admired any of his friends, there was an immediate response-Nah, with a shrug.

My oldest son, at 19, had a completely different approach than his younger brother. Thankfully both boys included their parents on their lists. Whew! Alex also included the parents of two of his friends. Both had developed multi-million dollar businesses from scratch. Neither parent was educated beyond high school. One of them was a single mother. Interestingly, neither of his friends, whose parents he admired, made his list. In fact, when I asked him if he admired any of his friends, I was met with the same immediate response that his younger brother gave -Nah! As if to say, they haven't done enough yet to earn my admiration.

As I looked more at who I admire, I realized what I admire most is not what those individuals had accomplished, but who they had to be in the process of those accomplishments. I admire how they lived their life and met challenges. I also realized that I don't spend much time with people I don't admire. I don't think it's been a conscious choice, but over time, I've filtered out all those relationships that don't give me something to grow into and to emulate. I believe I have also chosen to find something to admire in everyone I'm associated with. I find my life is richer that way.

As with just about everything I do these days, I looked to see how this applies to communication. For one thing, if we visualize ourselves demonstrating these qualities we admire (Remember we can't see them if we don't have them!), we present ourselves at our authentic best. This is important to note. Our authentic self is the most engaging, interesting, relatable person we can be! I'm not suggesting that you pretend you are a person with these qualities. There is no need to pretend. The qualities you have identified that you admire are qualities you possess. What I recommend is that you focus your attention on being those qualities.

If one of those qualities you've identified in several of the people you admire is humor, then ask yourself, "How would a humorous person approach this communication?" If you admire generosity, how would a generous person be in this presentation? One of the qualities I admire is energy, so I create my communication to reflect that authentic expression of myself. At first, it may feel awkward. Be patient with yourself. Give it time.

Chapter 3 Exercise

Who I Admire

1. In the first column, list the names of people you admire. These can be individuals you know personally, historical figures, famous individuals, even organizations.

2. List all the traits or characteristics about them you admire.

3. Scan the list of traits and circle the ones that show up a few times.

4. Put the circled traits in the column "Your authentic traits."

Name	Traits or Characteristics	Your Authentic Traits

The attributes in the final column, your authentic traits, will give you a sound foundation from which to communicate authentically.

Turning Up the Volume

Another way we miss the mark in "being" authentic in our communication is by being untrue to the authentic self. After we have become aware of that inner voice, it gets louder and louder, until it can finally be heard over the noise in our lives. Then we communicate the opposite. These are the times when we say, "I'm really excited to be here" when what we really mean is, "Boy this is the most boring thing I've ever been asked to do. How am I ever going to make it through this?" Or the more common "Is something wrong?" "Oh no. I'm fine."

Right now, you might be saying, "Oh great, you're going to tell me instead of being polite and smiling and telling people I'm excited to be speaking to their group, I'm supposed to tell the truth, hurt feelings, be rude and probably destroy my chances of ever being asked to speak to anyone again, all in the attempt to connect to my authentic self."

Well not exactly.

What it means is being yourself. Tap into and pay attention to what's really going on with you. Then, find the appropriate way to express it. It means paying attention to how you truly feel about your subject matter. This usually takes the form of where your passions and convictions lie. It means turning down the volume of the external sounds and turning up the volume of the inner voice. It's about paying attention-moment to moment.

For example, a Bravo client had just been named CEO to head up the merger of 2 large financial services companies. He was scheduled to make a speech welcoming everyone in the new company. His intention was to inspire the troops with excitement and a mission to go forward and conquer the world. As Chuck and I worked with him, he kept stepping back, just as he declared how excited he was about leading this new organization and how optimistic he was about the future. Whenever someone steps back when they make a declaration, it's a red flag that the statement is in some way untrue. Rather than coach him to stop stepping back, we asked "What is it about this situation you are not feeling excited about?" He insisted that he was feeling excited. So we played back the video tape of his step back for him to see. After some time, he confessed to being dismayed by the prospect that his role was going to change from interacting one on one with clients to being primarily responsible for managing a large company and its sales force.

This "dismay" was an authentic feeling that he was trying to mask with words, false words, and fake excitement. We coached him to tap into what was real for him and communicate that, rather than wear a mask that hid his true feeling about the matter. The truth is revealed in your communication anyway, in his case stepping back when making a statement that was untrue for him. Many times your body speaks louder than your words.

After spending some time taking a closer look at what he was actually apprehensive about, he took a different approach.

"I'm really excited by what these changes mean for our company. We have an opportunity to build on the strength we've demonstrated in the past and go forward with some real momentum. Quite frankly, this will mean some changes for all of us, some changes that may be difficult. I get a little apprehensive myself when I look at the change in roles I will be undertaking. In spite of this, I can honestly say the future looks great and I am committed to doing my part to seize this new opportunity."

He was able to express his true feelings, from the heart, authentically and with passion

Most of us tend to ignore or not be conscious of what we're really feeling. Too often, it's because we live on   automatic pilot, with life whizzing by us at warp speed, not taking the time to pay attention to what we're experiencing. As an individual, it may feel a bit self indulgent to think about yourself in such a focused way. Or, it could be frightening to look so closely at what's really going on. You may be afraid of what you might discover. Maybe you won't like what you see or find out about yourself. But then again, maybe you will like what you see. I believe we all have the opportunity to have richer, more complete experiences in our lives and as a result, become better communicators because we can share ourselves more completely.

.

CHAPTER 4

Communication Is All About Relationship

Before we can make friends with anyone else,
we must first make friends with ourselves.

Eleanor Roosevelt

Communication is all about relationship and the first relationship is with oneself. If we are not on intimate terms with ourselves, we can't be in a relationship with others. That's the exciting part. I find that delving into this kind of journey to get reacquainted with your self is like having a new exciting romance. You know how in the first few months of a love affair, everything is perfect. Even those things that later drive you crazy, at first are just cute little idiosyncrasies. Well maybe you can look at getting to know the real you in the same way. Discovering all the little quirks rather than ignoring or hiding them. Maybe you can view them as you would a new lover, with some interesting, cute quirks.

Deny, Deny, Deny

What happens to those who are conscious of their authentic self?

Some embrace it and enjoy a new found ease in their communication. Many others deny that self. Imagine you're now aware that you are really afraid to be in front of a group. Or you're aware that what you really believe just below the surface is that no one will like you. Now what do you do? Deny Deny Deny. We deny that we actually feel that way. I met a professional speaker who was very successful in the industry. He was speaking about 250 days a year and making about $7,500 for a one hour speech. Not bad. After we had too many cognacs at the end of a day long event, he asked me what I saw when he spoke. I told him I saw an 8 year old boy, terrified of the audience. He was surprised to hear my comment and was honest enough to tell me he, in fact, didn't believe that people would like him when he got up in the front of the room. His communication was being ruled by this impression of himself. He was denying his true self by living with the fear of who he thought he was. He was trying to mask over his fear of being rejected by acting like it didn't matter. My advice was to get clear on the value he was bringing to his audiences and start his speeches knowing that the audience was on his side, not there to shoot him at the first opportunity or to find him out.

Denial Is Suffering

Denial of who we are, especially when we have some insight into our true self, is suffering. To recognize that you are fearful of the people you're talking to and then to pretend that's not so, is suffering. One way he could have handled the situation was to first acknowledge his fear. "Wow, I see that old friend of mine, 'I don't think they'll like me', is back. OK what can I do about that? Well, first of all, know I have some valuable material to give them. I've got some good stories that will keep them engaged. And, you know what, some of them may not like me, but most of them will. Even if they don't like what I have to say doesn't mean I'm not a valuable person.

I'm just going to go and do the best I can, and they'll like me or they won't."

If he had that kind of confidence and willingness to be vulnerable, accept his fear and move through it, he would have been more present to being with his audience.

I experienced the suffering from denial in a situation with one of my children. My son was driving me crazy, misbehaving. This was taking place as we were doing a series of errands. We were in the bank, with lots of people standing in line and my son was acting out, racing up and down the bank trying to stay in the view of the security camera. I noticed I was becoming a little irate, but working hard to keep my cool. I transferred my upset with my son by expressing my irritation at the teller. To this point I was being extremely patient with my son, not communicating with him my upset, basically ignoring how I was feeling about his behavior. I was denying my upset, embarrassment, irritation, anger. He even kept asking me if I was embarrassed. I kept saying "No. Why would I be embarrassed? I'm not the one making a fool of myself." The truth was I was embarrassed and angry, and irritated by his antics. He continued this behavior. I have to give it to him for tenacity and perseverance. I still kept my cool, through the bookstore with the sales person at the check out saying something like, "Boy you must be glad school's out. A little too much sugar today?" I even held it during the trip to Toys R Us, though I knew I was close to the end, as I begged, "Please, let's go. I hate Toys R US." I finally let my real feelings come through at the linen store as I was looking at some new Egyptian cotton towels. My son began dismantling one of the displays. Not a big dismantling, just lying cards down that were placed upright. But I lost it. I finally broke through the denial of how I was truly feeling and lashed out by giving him a backhanded swat across the stomach to stop it. Well, that escalated into something else. I felt terrible because I slapped him. He was mad at being struck. All this happened because I denied that he was getting to me from the start. I denied what was real and it led to an inappropriate reaction by me and gave him the incentive to continue his behavior because he wanted, needed, a reaction from me. I've learned that kids have far more perseverance than parents or adults. I've noticed they also like to keep the game going so they can have control. The main point about this is that by denying what's real for you doesn't make it go away. It actually may just make it go underground until it builds up so much pressure that it explodes, like a volcano. Those are the times when you can do or say something you will regret.

I love it when someone says they're happy to see you and you look at their face and they look like Deputy Dog, the cartoon basset hound. My reaction is, tell your face! If you are feeling something, express it. If you're feeling happy, "be" happy. If you are feeling excited, "be" excited. If you're feeling outrage, "be" outraged. I was coaching a wonderful woman by the name of Carol who has created a business in Houston to feed starving children by setting up a program like Meals on Wheels for kids. As she delivered her speech to me initially, she spoke about her experience of seeing children eating out of garbage cans. She talked about her disgust at the filth these children were living in and her feeling that there must be something deficient about the parenting that allowed this to take place. She told stories about her mother who instilled in her sense of charity for people who had less, and her outrage at the city of Houston for shutting down her kitchen that was feeding the starving children of the city because she didn't have a mop sink or a vent hood for her stove. When we first began to work together, she told all these stories in the same, matter of fact tone. I coached her to express the emotion she felt authentically about each of these situations, to give each one their due, so that the real Carol would show through. When she delivered her talk to an audience of 7,000, the audience could see the disgust she felt at the smells and dirt that were commonplace for the children she was helping. Her righteous indignation toward the city officials was evident in her voice and posture. Her pride and love for her mother came through in her choice of words and her tone. Especially her excitement and passion for making a difference in the lives of Houston's starving children came through loud and clear. Making that little shift, of giving herself permission to be herself, opened up a way for Carol to be a much more powerful communicator.

Having your emotions without your emotions having you

When I say express how you're feeling authentically, it does not mean that if you are saddened by something, you fall apart and become incapacitated. No, it means don't deny what you're feeling by trying to pretend you feel something else or worse, nothing at all. It means having your emotions without your emotions having you, as my friend Stewart Emery said in his insightful book, Actualizations: You Don't Have to Rehearse To Be Yourself. Being present to how you feel, expressing the passion, the emotion, connects you with whoever your audience is. They have a real person to be in relationship with. Not a cardboard cut out of someone who gives only the mask.

Think of the people you've been moved by when you've received their communication or heard them speak. What do they have in common? Think of the ones you've been put off by. What is it about them that turns you off? Do you notice you feel more connected to the communicators who are authentic and feel like a "real" person?

The Barbeque Test

One of the tests I give people when they are attempting to be more authentic communicators is the backyard barbeque test. Imagine yourself in your backyard, talking to your neighbor (the one you really like, not the one you're in a dispute over the property line.). Imagine you're drinking a couple of beers, flipping the dogs and burgers and you're having a conversation, as friends do. The comfort level you have in expressing what you're really feeling, the conversational tone in this type of setting gives insight and guidance to how all your communication can go. You as the speaker must feel the freedom of being yourself, all yourself, not the stripped down version. You the speaker are not to be limited by who you think you're supposed to be, what everyone will like, or what's acceptable, but who you truly are, authentically. Trust that who you are is enough. Take comfort in the knowledge that when you communicate authentically, better results happen. How is that possible? There is a real person there to be in relationship with. Remember, communication is all about being in relationship. Some say that being in a relationship is all about communication. I don't disagree.

Chapter 4 Exercise

The intent of this exercise is to develop awareness of your authentic emotions. One of the easiest access points we have to our authentic feelings is through our past experiences. Often these experiences are pivotal is forming our direction and purpose in life while shaping our values. To do this exercise, sit quietly, with your eyes closed.

1. Scan your thoughts until you recall an experience from your past. Don't worry about coming up with the "right" memory. What ever comes up for you is perfect. It could be the first bike you bought with your own money. It could be learning how to make maple syrup, or ice fishing with your grandfather.

2. As you connect with that memory, still with your eyes closed, experience the incident with all your senses. What were the smells of the day? What were the sounds? Notice the season and temperature. See what you were wearing? How did your clothing feel on your skin? Notice the colors. Was anyone else with you? If so, who? What emotions were you feeling during that memory? Can you feel them now?

3. Describe the situation out loud, either to someone else or to yourself. Be as specific as possible, being aware of how you felt when this experience took place. Saying it out loud brings it back into focus, enabling connection to the experience. What was significant about this situation? What conclusions have your drawn from it?

4. Do this exercise several times, until you build confidence in your ability to fully experience and express your authentic emotions.

5. A complementary exercise for tapping into your authentic feelings is to write your personal history in a journal. Not only will it support the development of consciousness about your emotions, but it will also generate compelling stories for your presentations.

CHAPTER 5
Creativity

Flamenco is a traditional dance that originated with the gypsies from the region of Spain ruled by the Moors. It is intensely passionate story telling involving a guitarist and dancer. As the guitarist strums and begins telling his story, the dancer will begin to tap and stomp out the stresses. If she is inspired by the emotion in the playing and the story telling, she will make those emotions visible through her interpretation in her dance. If she is unmoved by the music or she lacks sufficient passion, she doesn't dance. Just like our audiences.

Flamenco is a great example of creative expression in dance. While few of us will ever be flamenco dancers, creativity is something we all possess. It isn't the exclusive domain of artists, poets, writers, musicians and actors. When you leave creativity only to "artists" you lose touch with your own inventiveness, and deny an avenue through which great energy and wisdom can make its way to you. It is possible that the only difference between the people you consider artists and yourself is the willingness to let your creative expression come out to play. That means listening to the sparks of intuition, those brilliant thoughts (yes, you do have brilliant thoughts!) that seem to come from no where. It means letting the doubts rest. Just as Michelangelo replied when asked about sculpting the David, he did not create the sculpture in marble. He only freed the form that was inside. Your expression in presentations means freeing the creativity you have inside.

The Critic, the Editor, and the Green Meanies

Do you hear voices in your head when you present? Don't worry. I won't send the men in white coats after you, but you know the voices I mean. The ones that tell you 'You're going to forget what to say next', 'Did you really think they'd laugh at that?' 'Why did you wear that suit?' 'They look bored' 'You're too old to be talking to them'.

There's an old joke that says, "Public speaking is the number one fear. Death is number two. That means that if you're at a funeral, you'd rather be the guy in the box than the one giving the eulogy." Those voices are what we really fear. Managing those voices is one of the biggest challenges in the speaking process.

All the negative comments are coming from what I call the Critic, the Editor, and the Green Meanies. We all have them, which is why I won't be sending the men in the white coats. Make no mistake about it though. They are not your friends. Listening to their litany will only undermine your confidence and send you on a downward spiral into the darkest regions of your mind, far away from your audience.

The Critics, Editor, and Green Meanies will feel threatened by the openness and enthusiasm in your expression of authentic self rather than the protected state of the speaker's persona and will attack with the viciousness of a cornered animal. They will leave you feeling lost and exposed, turning against yourself in self judgment. They are your built in backseat drivers, questioning every turn you make, direction you decide on. They will see things that aren't there, hear things that aren't said, and make their arguments with such conviction there will seem to be no counter argument. They do not play fair!

Their job is to keep you from the unfamiliar. Anything new is seen as a threat. That includes any creative thoughts, insights, innovations. Before you even complete a thought, their Greek chorus jumps in telling you all the reasons why it's the wrong thing to say, do or believe. There are a multitude of reasons why not, and why you should stay the course.

Right Brain Left Brain

Nobel Laureate, Roger Sperry pioneered the work with the different modes of thinking in the left and right hemispheres of the brain. In his ground breaking research, he discovered the realm of the left brain is one of logic and control. Its job is to recognize the familiar and to categorize. It has no interest in detailed perceptions.

The right hemisphere rules creative expression, intuition and insights. This is where great inspiring new ideas come from. It is said that The Theory of Relativity first occurred to Einstein as a tingling in his elbow. This kind of instinct or intuition is rejected by our rational brain because it cannot be measured or controlled. The strength of our logical left brain is so strong and is given so much more weight in our civilization, that it snaps us out of our right brain thinking unless we are willing to let go. Creativity and

> "I never came upon any of my discoveries through the process of rational thinking"
>
> —Albert Einstein

control cannot occupy the same space. They are mutually exclusive. Creativity is expansive while control is retractive by its very nature.

I recently experienced this while coaching a good friend who is an engineer by training. His years of study and professional practice have forced him to exercise the logical brain function while the creative, intuitive side has atrophied. I happen to know this man is a warm, funny, loving person under that logical exterior. As I was coaching him, I had a flash of inspiration. I remembered a short film from the 70's called Bambi Meets Godzilla. In the opening moments of the film, Bambi is seen in a pastoral setting, munching on grass, enjoying the serene spring day, when all of a sudden, Godzilla's big foot comes down and squashes Bambi. Then the final credits roll. I used this example with my friend to demonstrate what happens to his moments of insight and inspiration. I advised him to be attentive to when the big foot of his logical brain was ready to take over and think "Run Bambi Run!"

But I'm Really Not Creative

It would be really easy to write off your creative capabilities because of the heavy muscle of your rational abilities, but we all have creative thoughts, more than we give ourselves credit for. Those thoughts frequently get discounted as silly, unimportant, a waste of time (that's the Critic talking!?) It may look like doodling while you're talking on the phone, or singing to a CD in the car, dancing in the living room when no one is watching. Or it could simply be daydreaming of a life that doesn't exist for you right now. All of these are creative expressions.

You may have thoughts of not feeling creative or inspired, as if you need to 'feel' creative to 'be' creative. This deeply ingrained conditioning stops you from creative expression. Most of us have the mistaken impression that creative people always feel creative and that it is easy for them.

I was driving to our family cabin in Northern Michigan to work on my first book, The Power to Connect, and feeling a little over- whelmed by the task. Coincidently, on the drive, I was listening to Anna Quindlin being interviewed about being a writer. In the inter- view she spoke about the challenges she faces everyday writing her columns and books, of finding excuses for not writing (the New York Times had to be read one more time, the laundry had to be folded) before the writing could take place. In the end, she said, writers write, whether they want to or not, whether they feel like it or not. Writers write. That was a well timed insight for me as I was strug- gling to find my inspiration.

You may think that your creativity lies outside yourself when it is really the expression of something deep within yourself. It is a process that takes practice and intuition. It's tapping into that part of yourself that gets neglected when you choose the safer course of logic and the known. Listen to those flashes of ideas. They are filled with discovery and insight. Often those spontaneous inspirations are disregarded as frivolous noise, when they are frequently the gems your audience will remember. When you treat your creative abilities seriously and with respect, you will see that there is intelligence in these suggestions. They are the core of your brilliance.

One of the classic books on tapping into the creative side is Betty Edward's "Drawing on the Right Side of The Brain." Whether or not you aspire to be an artist, the exercises included in her instruction are tremendous for training your eyes to see differently, exercising the right brain capabilities.

Also, Judith Cameron has written several books on tapping into your creative abilities. Her best known is "The Artist's Way" and is a great resource for unleashing the creative within.

My invitation is to exercise your creativity and strengthen that muscle so you have the confidence that it's always at your disposal.

Prepare And You Will Be Set Free

The Critic, the Editor, and the Green Meanies will continue their barrage of advice and comments until you provide a safe situation for them. The way to quiet those voices is ironically by utilizing the rational: preparation. By preparing thoroughly, you can tell the chorus to go take a nap. You have things under control. When that crowd leaves because it's satisfied it's secure, the creative side can find greater expression.

> *"Did you ever observe to whom accidents happen?*
> *Chance favors only the prepared mind"*
>
> **—Louis Pasteur**

I've witnessed some resistance from speakers when I tell them that preparation is necessary to be more creative. They'll say, 'I'm better when I wing it. I'm more spontaneous.' Well, sometimes, but it's a high wire act. Sooner or later if you insist on winging it, you go SPLAT!

It's through preparation that creativity is freed. Preparation enables you to focus entirely on the audience, reading their responses, and having the intuitive thought that tells you, "This is the perfect story here. This is the example that will make this all clear."

Being fully prepared in advance doesn't mean you don't get to be spontaneous. It's preparation that actually facilitates your ability to respond to a situation. It's only by mapping the entire presentation out, knowing what's going to happen next, that you have the freedom to create something different in the moment, being in a dance with your audience. Winging it means you must constantly be thinking on your feet about what to say or do next. When you're listening to yourself, you're not listening to your audience. That's where all your results come from, your audience.

The two templates included in the "Doing" part of the book were created by Chuck and me to support our clients in preparing for all their presentations. We recommend, strongly I might add, that you use these.

Chapter 5 Exercise

For Strengthening Creative Capabilities

Anything that our logical brain can't or won't do will allow the intuitive part to be exercised. These are things we can't "think" our way through. In Bravo Presentation Coaching, we have several improvisational exercises that require the abandonment of logic and reason to complete them successfully. You also may want to enroll in an improve class. Comedy clubs like Second City frequently offer classes to develop not only your comedic abilities, but your channel for intuition and inspiration.

Engage in creative pursuits. Drawing or painting expands our capability to visualize. Writing develops our story telling and ability to create imagery. Dance increases our range of motion and confidence in physical expression. Pursuing any of these is not necessarily for the show or recital. Participating in anything that helps you pay more attention to your life and connect to your authentic self will strengthen your intuition, innovation and creativity. Things like daily journaling, meditation, music, long walks, art, marshal arts, and yoga are also included.

There are also some simple techniques that can help us practice the shift from logic brain to creative brain. They are designed to "switch" the neural pathways in our brain to get more cooperation and balance.

Exercise 1

This is an eye exercise. It's very simple and can be done in the safety of your own home, far from the view of anyone who may think you're nuts for doing it. Move your eyes several times from side to side. Then move your eyes in a big circle without moving your head. First move them clock wise several times. Then switch to a counter clock wise movement. You may feel a jerky motion as you make the circles. As the movement smoothes, there is a smoother transfer of information between the rational left brain and creative right parts of the brain. (Strange but true.)

Exercise 2

This exercise is done standing up. Some of you who have taken aerobics classes will recognize it. In this case, you don't have to get out your sweats and sneakers though! Lift your left knee and meet it with your right elbow. Switch and meet your right knee with your left elbow. Do this several times until there is a fluidity of motion. This exercise, like the eye exercise before, is designed to break the log jam of thinking between rational and intuitive.

CHAPTER 6

Connection

"Your audience gives you everything you need.
They tell you. There is no director who
can direct you like an audience."

Fanny Brice

It's Not About You

For connection to take place, it requires placing your attention squarely where it belongs, on the other person. We all crave connection. In fact, connection is as important to our well being as food and water. Studies have shown that orphaned infants who are fed, clothed, cleaned and kept warm but not held, played with, or cuddled become sickly, withdrawn, lose weight, and many die. The customs of hugging upon arrivals and departures is a result of that same instinct for connection with others.

Authentic communication forges a bond between the speaker and the audience. It recognizes the affiliation we have for one another and builds on our desire for relationship. The fear and anxiety speakers experience is the retreat away from connection. It is the inward focus on self rather than the outward focus on others. When you're listening to yourself, you can't hear anyone else. Without care, there is no relationship, no connection between you and your audience. The thread of feeling that links you to your audience is the most precious thing of all; it is the conduit through which your energy passes.

I'm Falling!

When the Critic, Editor and Green Meanies begin their chorus, the most common reaction is to continue down the tunnel, following their siren's voices further into your head. Just like when you lose your balance, the way to recover is to counter the motion by going in the opposite direction. When the voices get loud and the fear begins to rise, the way out is counter intuitive. Put your attention where there is safety and support, on your audience, away from yourself.

The Audience Is On Your Side

Audiences start out on your side. They want you to win. Having a speaker stumble and fail leaves an audience with an experience that has wasted their time or worse, reminded them too much of their own "character building" experiences. When the audience sees you suffer as a speaker, they feel it too. I'm not talking about those rare occasions or individuals who relish or hope to cause discomfort for a speaker. I'm talking about the vast majority of audiences you will be speaking to.

The Triune Brain

To better understand how to connect with your audience, it's helpful to understand how the brain works. Human beings place a greater weight on logical, rational capabilities, yet we make our decisions based on emotions. This is supported by some of the most recent studies on brain functionality. Neurophysiologist, Dr. Paul McLean identified what is now referred to as the triune brain or three part brain. The human brain is comprised of: the reptilian brain, the limbic brain, and the neocortical brain. Each part has a distinct function and makes a significant contribution to our lives.

The Reptilian Brain

The reptilian brain is the oldest part of our brain from an evolutionary stand point. This is the part that was critical during times of physical threats like carnivorous animals who felt they were higher on the food chain. It's the 'flight or fright' part of our brain that would instantly interpret waving tall grass as meaning a predator was near and flight or fright action was called for. This is the brain that controls involuntary body function too-breathing, heart rate, digestion-the basic functions.

The Limbic Brain

The second part of the brain to evolve was the limbic brain. It is the part of the brain where emotional connections are made. In fact, this is the part that controls nurturing and relationships. It's also the part where intuition, creativity, and verbal communication take place. Our ability to "read" one another's facial expressions is no mystery. Studies have shown that facial expressions are the same and are "factory installed" equipment for humans across all cultures and geography. There is no culture that shows happiness by turning the corners of the mouth down or squinting the eyes when surprised. Studies have also shown that babies with congenital blindness will smile when they hear their mother's voice, even though they have never seen a smile.

They Are Paying Attention

Your audience "gets" your communication loud and clear from the minute you make your entrance, whether it's on the stage, in the boardroom, in the office lobby, or over the table in the dining room. What you forget is that you are always communicating. In fact, you are incapable of not communicating. It's like breathing. You are a perfect communication machine. Let me repeat that because we all feel like we are imperfect in our communication abilities. You are a PERFECT communication machine. Your body does not lie. It is a direct channel for what is going on in your thoughts. And, it is available for your audience to see. It can be seen in your posture, your choice of clothing, the tone of your voice, your choice of words and how you move. You may not be conscious of what you're communicating, but you're transmitting none the less. Various studies estimate that between 70-95% of our communication is non verbal.

Take this example. You are at the mall to purchase a new pair of shoes for your child. As you are walking toward the exit, you see a young man in his late teens coming toward you. You immediately notice the tattoos covering both of his arms and especially the one wrapping from the back of his neck to his throat. You also can't miss the multitude of piercings in his face, eye brows, ears and nose or the chains draping down from his black pants and boots. As he passes, he bumps your shoulder hard enough for you to nearly drop your packages. You immediately spin around, jaw tightened, fists clenched, eyes narrowed, shoulders drawn up. He continues on his way, paying no attention to you. In the meantime, following behind this youth is an attractive person of the opposite sex who has seen the entire incidence. You look at one another, smile, sigh, shake your head, shrug, and continue on your way. In those 15 seconds, a tremendous amount of communication took place, all of it non verbal. All of it easily understood to someone paying attention. How many of us with children have any confusion about the communication in the rolling of the eyes and a sigh?

The Neo Cortical Brain

The third part of the brain is the neo cortical. This is where logic, verbal language, and abstract thinking reside. This is the part of our brain that has given us the internet, television, microwaves and cell phones. For these reasons alone, we may want to get a lobotomy! It's the newest part of the brain and separates us from the rest of the animal kingdom. Because it gives us our advantage over other creatures, we tend to place more emphasis on its capabilities and treat the other parts of the brain as inferior. We have a mistaken idea that the logic can rule, can bend those other brains to its will. That's like trying to will your self to love someone. You may be able to control your behavior, but control your emotions. That's another story when you get two parts of the brain with different ideas.

In fact, the triune brain is not a hierarchy. All parts work together on an equal footing. You cannot survive without the function of the reptilian brain. If the limbic and neocortical functions are damaged or removed, a person can still operate, though they are in a state called 'brain dead'. An example of having only neocortical brain functionality is Mr. Spock from Star Trek. He's a good guy to have around, but missing the whole picture.

The story of Archimedes is an example that demonstrates the importance of using the limbic part of our brain in communication. Archimedes was a mathematician about 2200 years ago. He was responsible for coming up with what is now called the Archimedes Principle, which states that the amount of water displaced by an object is equal to its weight. While this principle is exciting to mathematicians, most of us are left cold by its logic. It appeals purely to the neocortical portion of our brain. Now listen to the story of how Archimedes arrived at his conclusion. According to legend, the king received a crown that was purported to be made of solid gold. The king had some doubt as to its authenticity. He commissioned Archimedes to figure out how he could determine if the crown was gold without melting it down. It is said that as Archimedes lowered himself into his bath, he realized that the amount of water displaced was equal to his weight and the same principle applied to the crown. Archimedes was so excited by his new discovery that, it is said, he ran naked through the streets, shouting "Eureka!" Thus giving birth to that famous exclamation.

While the principle of physics Archimedes discovered is interesting to those who are so inclined, it's not the most memorable part of the story. What gets our attention is the naked man running through the street, shouting Eureka! In fact most of you will forget what the Archimedes Principle is, if you haven't already forgotten. You may even forget the author was Archimedes, but you will remember the guy running through the street yelling "Eureka" as the origin of that expression.

What does this have to do with your presentation? Most of us believe that if we provide more and better information that, logically, people will be moved to take the action we want. In fact, more information tends to confuse the issue. People make decisions based on your ability to inspire them, to show them you have shared experiences with them, and that you have a course of action that leads them to make progress. I have found people don't expect you to have all the answers. They do expect you to provide direction that comes from your passion and conviction. This is the first step to being heard above the crowd. Speak from your passion, conviction and commitments. When you begin there, you can create an emotional connection with your audience.

Passion & Conviction

When we attempt to motivate an audience to take action, accept our point of view, follow our mandate or change behaviors, we often will try to influence them with reason, dispassionately. What causes people to be convinced is your passion and conviction. That you believe what you are saying and express it, will serve you better than all the logical arguments you can come up with.

If you want to inspire people to do something, you must feel passion and conviction and appeal to the emotions of your audience. In the presidential campaign between George W. Bush and John Kerry, Senator Kerry did not consistently demonstrate his passion and conviction. After the election, the commentators consistently talked about his inability to connect. That's because he was trying to connect at a cerebral level and missed the emotional. The cost, the Presidency.

You may not be running for President, but communicating what is important to you, from the heart, will move you far along the path of what you hope to accomplish.

Part Two

DOING

CHAPTER 7

The Power To Connect

In our Bravo Presentation Coaching Program, we recommend that every presentation begin with a communication strategy. Chuck and I created a template specifically designed to assist in that strategic thinking. For those who have read our book, The Power to Connect, or attended one of our workshops, this will be familiar. In both the book and the workshop, we go into this process and the thinking behind it in depth. In fact, it is the basis of the methodology we have devised for our consulting, the communication tools we create, and the projects we execute for our clients at Corporate Vision Communications.

This may seem like pretty basic stuff, yet there is sophistication in its simplicity. By focusing on these 8 important topics, you will be better prepared and as a result be more present and connected with your audience.

Who Is Your Audience?

The purpose of this section dedicated to the audience is to support you in breaking the gravitational pull of being at the center of the universe. It forces you to put your attention fully on the audience. While we all like to think we speak with our audience in mind, in fact we habitually speak from our own point of view. When I hear speakers defend their position "I always focus on the audience" it sends up red flags. These are the speakers who are so immersed in seeing things from their own stand point they no longer recognize or consider that someone else may see things differently. None of us can focus on the audience 100% of the time. We're just not built that way. We need all the support we can get to change that focus.

The place to begin is who is your audience? It seems like a simple question, yet it is one most of us don't seriously look at when we begin crafting our speeches, especially if they are people we have spoken to before. They may be similar to the audiences we have spoken to in the past or they are clients. Because there is familiarity, we paint them with a broad brush and miss out on the opportunity to really think about who we are presenting to.

As you describe your audience, start broadly: gender, age, stage of career. Then work your way into more detail: personality, concerns, aspirations, modes of operating. Keep going until you have as much detail as you can get so when you begin your presentation, you feel like you're talking to people you know, friends. Remember, presentations are all conversations and who better to converse with than friends. Breaking down the barrier of "them" and "me" will help you be more connected, lower the volume of your personal Greek Chorus: the Critic, Editor, and Green Meanies.

> "Proclaim not all thou knowest."
>
> —Benjamin Franklin

What 3 Things Do I Want My Audience To Remember After They Leave The Presentation?

Let's begin with what you want your audience to remember. What are the three things you want your audience to remember at the end of your presentation? The first question many people ask is why only three things, especially when you have so many important things for them to remember. It's very simple. You can't rely on your audience to remember more than three things. You can have fewer than three, but more is a no no.

The audience already has too much information to shift through on a daily basis, so adding more doesn't support them in making a decision. It may even delay action. To give you an idea of how much information we have to sort through and categorize as important or non-essential, here are a few facts:

Some scientist are now saying that it takes less time to do an experiment than to see if the same experiment has been done before.

In every 24 hour period, approximately 20 million words of technical information are being recorded. A reader capable of reading 1,000 words per minute would need 45 days, reading 8 hours a day to get through one day's worth on new technical output. At the end of that period he would have fallen 5.5years behind in his reading!

More new information has been produced in the last three decades than in the last five millennia.

The amount of information published between 1999 and 2002 equals that of all prior recorded history.

It's no surprise then that while you are speaking, the audience is trying to figure out quickly and easily which information is useful, which is not, and what they should remember from everything you have to say.

> "The secret of being boring is to tell everything."
>
> —Voltaire

> "Talk to a man
> about himself
> and he will
> listen for hours."
>
> —Benjamin Disraeli

So when choosing the three things you want your audience to remember, it must make it through this filter. Here's how you get your information through the filter. Answer for your audience two critical questions: 'What's in it for me?' and 'Why do I care?' When you answer these two questions, the message will make it into your audiences "real need" category of information rather than the "that's interesting" disposable file. If your three things don't answer these questions, go back to the drawing board.

How Do I Want My Audience To Feel At The End Of My Presentation?

Next comes, "How do I want my audience to feel at the end of my presentation? Since they're going to feel something anyway, you might as well decide beforehand the emotional experience you plan to create with your presentation. If you're wondering why we included this in the strategic thinking part of preparation, the answer is simple and familiar. People make decisions based on emotion and justify it with the facts. As I covered in the discussion on connection, we are all looking for that emotional relationship and its authentic expression. To think your audience's decisions and actions will take place because they have all the facts is erroneous.

Have you ever made a significant purchase based on emotion, your home for instance? You walked in and it just felt right. You could see yourself and your family there enjoying it. You could imagine having friends over, celebrating the holidays. Then of course, you did your due diligence to make sure it was a sound purchase, but the sale was already made. The fact that it was in the right neighborhood, the school system was good, and it was an easy commute to work were the icing on the cake.

As a case in point, one of my colleagues recently purchased a new car shortly after buying a new home. She impressed upon me that she and her husband were being very logical and dispassionate about their car purchase. They went with mid range car with limited options because of their recent home purchase. They were being very rational about not over extending themselves financially. We were talking shortly after the car purchase when she told me the car was in the shop. Surprised, I asked what was wrong since it was brand new. "Oh, we're having a spoiler put on the back." I just laughed and said, "So much for logical, rational purchasing!" Do you think that decision was driven by emotion?

We all make these decisions from what we now know is the limbic region of the brain. Since we know that's how decisions are made, it makes sense to consider it when we're crafting our presentations.

What Action Do I Want My Audience To Take After Hearing Me Speak?

Many of us don't really think about what we want, so it should be no surprise when we don't get it! By thinking carefully about this in advance of your presentation, guess what, the chances are greater that your audience will actually do what you want. Be specific in the action you desire. "Who does what by when?" When you leave the action open-ended with no time frame attached, you create "doing leaks", ways for the audience not to take action. It would be like telling your kids to clean their room but not when you want it clean. There's always later!

> "In any moment of decision the best thing you can do is the right thing, the next best thing is the wrong thing, and the worst thing you can do is nothing,"
>
> —Teddy Rooseveldt

I hear speakers express their concern about being direct in telling audiences what they would like them to do. They are apprehensive about appearing too pushy, intrusive, or salesy because they are being so direct by asking for what they want. I don't think that will happen. First of all, if you have made your case, doing what you request is a natural next step. As speakers, we make the assumption that our audience knows what to do next, so we don't have to tell them. That isn't always the case, so letting them know how to proceed if they are interested is a service. Secondly, by being direct and asking for what you want, when you want it, you give the audience three choices: they can agree to do what you ask, they can decline, or they can renegotiate the time frame or the specific action. Any of those results is preferable to "I'll think about it" or inertia.

One other note on the "Action" section. Thinking is not an action. If it stays between your ears, it doesn't happen in the physical world. That means, as part of your strategy, you don't write down that you'd like them "to think about their circumstances and how your product/service would positively impact it." Or "Think about contributing to our charity." My favorite is one I heard while driving and listening to National Public Radio during a pledge period. The announcer came on and thanked all the members who had given generously (so far so good) and asked the listeners who had not contributed to think about it. As I was driving, I kept saying to myself, I'm thinking about it. Thinking. Thinking. Thinking. I'm not picking up my phone and giving a credit card number or writing a check, but I'm thinking about it. I did exactly what they requested but they didn't get the result. I wondered how many other people driving did the same thing, only thought about it. Thinking isn't going to close the deal. Action will.

What Is It You Appreciate About Your Audience?

This is one of the most powerful questions you can answer when preparing for your speech. Your opinion of your audience affects how you speak to them, how you treat them, and how you expect them to respond to you. Your perceptions and judgments of them will color everything you say, how you hold our body, the tone of your voice.

Dr. Masaru Emoto has conducted a fascinating study of the impact positive and negative thoughts have on water crystals. In his book "The Hidden Messages in Water" Dr. Emoto shows photographs of various water crystals. Water that is exposed to positive words develops beautiful colorful snowflake patterns while water exposed to negative words and thoughts develops incomplete, damaged forms. Since our bodies are 70% water, it's not so difficult to believe that our thoughts of appreciation toward our audience can have an impact on them. To begin your presentation from a place of honest appreciation connects you with your audience, limiting further any divide between speaker and audience.

One caution with appreciation. If what you appreciate about your audience has anything to do with you, for instance, they took the time to hear you speak, it's about you and not about them. This question is to be answered as if you weren't in the picture. Remember, it's not about you!

What Are The Predisposed Attitudes And Conditions In The Room To Be Addressed To Open The Channel For Communication?

Rarely does anyone get a perfectly clear channel for communication when they are speaking. There is always static in the line to consider. Some of the static may be attitudes the audience brings to the situation. They may think that accountants are boring, attorneys are sharks, financial advisors only want to sell them something, or all politicians are dishonest. If you are a CPA, attorney, financial advisor, or politician, these are definitely attitudes that could get in the way of the audience hearing what you have to say. The more you can identify these attitudes in advance, the better your chance of having a clear channel. As you design your presentation, you can do this directly by acknowledging the attitude or you can counter the attitude by demonstrating the opposite.

With conditions that could block your communication channel, anticipation is still the best approach. I tell my clients that I can guarantee that if they use technology (For example, PowerPoint, microphones, video) that it will not work. I don't know when exactly it won't work, but sooner or later, it will fail, so plan for that eventuality. I was speaking to a group of 2,000 entrepreneurs when my lapel microphone stopped working as soon as I took the stage. This was after numerous technical checks and re checks. I ended up having to use a hand held microphone for the entire 90 minute speech. For someone who is an animated speaker like me, this created a real hindrance

One of the wildest situations I heard about was with a Bravo client who was speaking to a group of financial advisors at a meeting in Park City, Utah. As soon as my client began his presentation, one of the men in the audience suffered from a Grand Mal seizure, so the entire group was moved to a new room. Unfortunately, the new room had a picture window behind the speaker that gave a panoramic view of the slopes, with skiers racing past them. Talk about distracting! But it didn't stop there. In the middle of the presentation, two chipmunks started chasing each other around the room! Now there was some static in the communication lines.

While these kinds of circumstances can't be anticipated, by eliminating as many of the preventable obstacles as possible makes the extraordinary situations easier to handle.

What do you have to say that will benefit your audience?

This question is a little tricky. It focuses on your presentation specifically, rather than the benefits of your product or services. The intent is to have you focus on always providing value when you speak, leaving you're audience with the sense that their time with you was time well spent, whether they take the action you request or not. Ironically, by having your attention on always creating value whenever you speak, the odds of the audience doing what you ask go up.

Who Do You Need To Be?

The immediate answer is authentic. Remember all those traits you wrote that describe the authentic you? Which of those is required for this specific presentation? Is this the place for the energetic you, the focused, directive you? Is this a speech that requires the playful you in order to get the results? Look at the 360° authentic you and choose the traits that will support getting the result you identified in the action section.

Title

When you are presenting publicly, your speech will need a title. There are a few rules of thumb to follow to ensure you have a title that compels people to come to hear you speak. Think of the title as your 30 second commercial, which has to engage the audience quickly. I recommend having seven words or fewer that grab the audience's attention. I like titles that are a little provocative or leave me wanting to hear more. I've heard more bad titles than good, unfortunately. For examples of what not to do, just go to the business section of the newspaper anywhere and look at the financial seminars being offered. "Managing Mutual Funds for a Secure Future" Yawn. "Your 401K and You" Snore. While I'm poking fun at these titles, I acknowledge there is a real talent to creating titles for speeches. If you do not feel confident in your own ability to come up with a title, I suggest hiring a writer to create one for you.

Before designing any presentation, think through this strategy completely. Write down your answers. Be clear about what you want to accomplish.

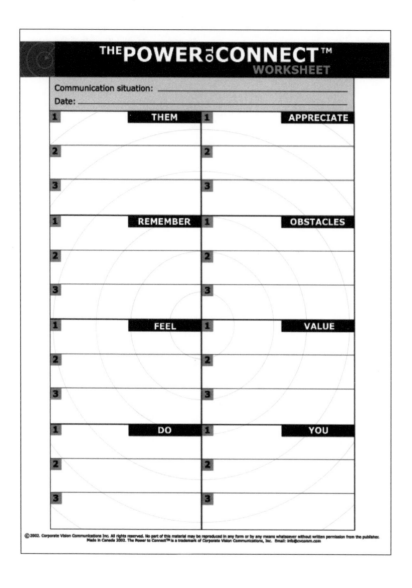

THE POWER to CONNECT™
WORKSHEET

Communication situation: _____

Date: _____

THEM	APPRECIATE
1	1
2	2
3	3

REMEMBER	OBSTACLES
1	1
2	2
3	3

FEEL	VALUE
1	1
2	2
3	3

DO	YOU
1	1
2	2
3	3

CHAPTER 8

Presentation Design

Superior presentations require developing skills in three technical components: clear, simple structure, development of rich memorable content, and finally, the impactful delivery of the material. The "doing" part of any presentation is a skill some can master, and everyone can improve. As with any skill, to get better requires practice and preparation.

In the years I've coached executives and entrepreneurs in their skills, I've noticed that everyone has a higher level of development in one of these components. Some have a talent for clearly structuring their presentation, while their content may be dry and their delivery uninspiring. Those with memorable   content frequently ramble and fail to have a cohesive presentation. The ones who have their delivery down pat often are the ones leaving us hungry at the end of the presentation, entertained but without substance. Building your skills to a level of excellence requires mastering all three components: structure, content, and delivery.

CHAPTER 9

Structure

If you have an important point to make,
don't try to be subtle or clever.
Use a pile driver. Hit the point once.
Then come back and hit it again.
Then hit it a third time a tremendous whack.

Winston Churchill

Let's begin with structure. The structure we recommend in our Bravo Presentation Coaching program has been around for centuries. In fact, it is the basis of Socratic debate. In modern times, it was popularized by advertising great, David Ogilvy. That structure is:

- Tell them what you're going to tell them.
- Tell them.
- Tell them what you told them.

There are other structures for presentations, but I like this one because of its simplicity and effectiveness in getting the results you desire. It's also prevalent in our everyday life. For example, the news magazine programs begin with, "Tonight, on Dateline" followed with a listing of the stories that will be covered on the show. That's the "Tell them what you're going to tell them" part. The show then goes in depth with the stories. That's the "Tell them" part. That's followed by the wrap up, with the montage and credits, which is the "Tell them what you told them" part. This is followed by a Call to Action, specifically, letting the audience know what to do next. "Tune in next week when we will be looking at...."

You will see this structure used in a variety of situations where there is a lot at stake. High profile cases like the OJ Simpson trial and the television program Law and Order are excellent demonstrations of how it is used in the courtroom every day. The prosecution tells the jury what they're going to prove in their opening statements (Tell them what you're going to tell them); "We will prove without a shadow of doubt that the defendant committed the crime he is accused of." This is followed by the presentation of the evidence and witnesses to prove the case (Tell them). Finally, the closing statements and the call to action (Tell them what you told them) are presented. "Ladies and gentlemen of the jury, we have shown that the accused had a motive and presented evidence with eyewitness testimony placing him at the scene of the crime. We ask you to deliver a verdict of guilty."

This structure is common and familiar. As a result, it's easy for your audience to relate to, follow, and assimilate your content. In a presentation, the "Tell them what you're going to tell them" part is the Open of your presentation. Its purpose is to engage your audience, to get their attention. I hear from many speakers that they're really good, once they get warmed up. That's too bad, because an audience is already onto the next thing they're thinking about, if you haven't gotten their attention right away. Of course, then you have to keep it. The intention of the Open is to immediately grab your audience by the shirt and don't let go. This will be covered in more depth in the discussion on creating memorable content. Audiences are making decisions about you, the speaker, in the first few seconds of your presentation. Some say the evaluation is completed in the first 5-7 seconds. If they're not engaged right away, you've lost them. You can win them back, but you're now in a defensive position and it's an uphill battle.

The "Tell them" part is the Body of the presentation. Its purpose is to build your case. This is where you add the information that leads to and supports your conclusions or beliefs. This is where you make it clear that to have a belief different from yours doesn't make sense. This is where you lead the audience to the action you want them to take, as a logical outcome of your presentation.

The "Tell them what you told them" part is the Recap. Its purpose is to reinforce what you've said up to this point. Most of the people I've coached and spoken to over the years have short attention spans and poor memories. Recapping is a service to help people remember and re-contextualize the information, ideas and emotions they have felt, seen, and heard in your presentation.

Finally, the Close. This is your Call to Action, letting your audience know specifically, Who- does What- by When. Don't waste the momentum you've created up to this point. Follow through. Support your audience in benefiting from what you have presented to them.

Warning! Some speakers have a tendency to go straight to the Body of the presentation. After all, that's where the meat is. Or, they'll start with an Open and develop the Body, but time will have a funny way of running out and they dump the Recap or Call to Action. This is a big reason speakers don't get the results they want. They don't remind their audience of what they're saying and don't let them know what they're supposed to do next. Make sure you practice and time your presentation to include all parts of the structure.

Sharp Transitions

Effective leaders communicate with great clarity. One of the most important keys to not having a fuzzy, wandering, unstructured presentation is to make clear when you have completed one thought or topic and that you are beginning another. Think of them like road signs that keep your audience going in the right direction with you, throughout the presentation. So at the end of the Open, let your audience know you're moving onto the Body. It can be as simple as saying "Let's begin", "Moving on to ...", or "We've finished exploring that topic, now let's look at..." Don't make this complicated. That's one of the pitfalls befalling speakers. They make the presentations far more complicated than necessary and wonder why their audiences are confused. Sharp transitions bring clarity to your speech, make it easier for your audience to follow, and make it easier for you to remember.

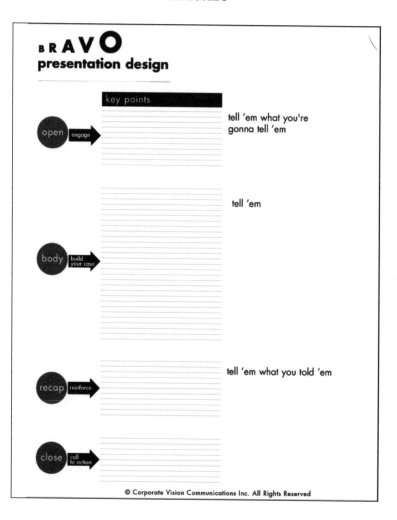

CHAPTER 10

Going Without A Crutch

Before we move on to creating memorable content, I'm going to vent for a moment. One of my biggest pet peeves with today's presenters is the over use of PowerPoint. Some have even accused me of being anti PowerPoint. Let me set the record straight here and now. I have nothing against PowerPoint. In fact, I use it myself for some of my workshops, and our company, Corporate Vision, creates PowerPoint presentations for some of our clients. What I do get annoyed by is the misuse of the technology. Instead of being a visual aid for the audience, as it was intended, it has become a crutch that has replaced preparation by the speaker. It has become a distraction when the speaker should be connecting with his audience. I've seen far too many speakers who virtually have their entire presentation, script and all, on PowerPoint slides. The presentation then becomes a reading exercise, with the speaker's back to the audience, reading slides. Ugh! Everyone who is reading this book has witnessed this, and some of you (I'm not naming names) are among the culprits. You know who you are! When I said PowerPoint is a visual aid, I meant it's a visual aid for the audience, not the speaker. The speaker should be prepared enough to not need the slides to keep him on track. The question then becomes, "What's the correct use for PowerPoint?"

It's good for reinforcing key points. It's excellent for illustrating a process, sophisticated concepts or complex relationships with drawings. It's appropriate to use to reveal the insight available in data with graphs. Having said that, complicated graphs and charts with fonts so small your audience would need binoculars to read are pointless. Also, the use of a graph without interpretation in a presentation is useless. An audience member will not be able to look at a graph, with lines jutting out, miniscule print explaining the X and Y axis, plus all the notes at the bottom, and be able to comprehend its significance at a glance. It requires explanation and interpretation. Remember, leaders communicate with clarity. They do not create confusion.

Since most of you will be using PowerPoint for your presentations, here are a few tips on how to use it effectively.

Teresa's Power Point Rules

Rule #1
No more than three bullet points per page

Rule #2
Have the points build, rather than all appear at once

Rule #3
Use the largest font size possible. If your grandmother can't read it at the back of the room, it's too small.

Rule #4
Use a consistent design template.

Rule #5
Be careful of gimmicky animation techniques and clip art –it distracts

Rule #6
Use colors that make it easy to read

Rule #7
Add interest, experience, and emotion by using icons, images, illustrations, and photographs.

Rule #8
Embed video clips when budget permits.

So, if you aren't supposed to use PowerPoint as your safety net then how do you remember everything you have to say? How do you prevent, the terror of all terrors, forgetting what you're supposed to say? The easy answer is preparation and practice. The more useful advice is how to practice and prepare. That brings us back to structure. When you have a simple structure to follow, remembering what you're going to say next, and being able to get back on track if you do veer off course is easy. Let go of your notes. You are the expert on your topic. You know everything you need to say.

Your Outline

Break the entire presentation into its outline form. Then memorize the outline. Most speakers present material they know well and may even be experts in. So, preparation isn't as much about learning something new as it is presenting what you already know and believe, in a manner that expresses your conviction and passions and captures your knowledge.

Here is an easy way for you to memorize just enough to give you the confidence you need to let go of the detailed notes or a word for word script. Chuck first used this approach to support a client who was preparing to deliver a new technology presentation at a major international trade show. His presentation was given twice every hour in his company's booth. The presentation theatre had a 12 foot rear projection screen, stereo sound, seating for 75, with standing room for another 100. In addition to his presence as the featured speaker, a live software demonstration, video clips, and supporting PowerPoint were integrated. This client was one of the founders of the breakthrough technology that changed the computer graphics industry. He was an icon. He knew more about the industry than anyone, with the exception of only a handful of people. Yet he was stressed by the complexities of the presentation and was anxious about forgetting something.

Chuck coached him to see the presentation from a different point of view. "Rather than focusing on this transfer of important data and detailed information, shift your focus to sharing what you know, and your personal experience." This gave the software guru a real life, story-like outline to speak from, which he was intimately familiar with. He was the authority. Establishing this context took away a lot of the complexity and made the data and details a lot easier to recall in a very natural way. He wasn't coached to be someone he was not, a professional speaker. He just had to be himself and deliver what he knew.

You may feel vulnerable without the complexity of detailed information and data, but it will make it easier for your audience to follow and take action.

So the first thing is to create an outline of your presentation. This outline will contain the information you will want to convey in a logical sequence that flows. This is a good time to evaluate your information to ensure it supports the three things you want your audience to remember from your Power to Connect worksheet.

Chapter 10 Exercise

List all the information you would like to include. Move it around so the flow is logical and causes the audience to want to know what's next.

CHAPTER 11

CONTENT

If information was all there was to your presentation, and for many it is, it would cause your audience to go to sleep or at least have their eyes glaze over. Having a strictly information based presentation leads to boredom. I know some of you are thinking that the type of business presentations you're giving are only information and it is boring, so what do you do to get around that?

In every Bravo Presentation Coaching program, we ask each participant to share a memorable presentation they have witnessed with the group and tell what made it memorable. In all the years I've been coaching, with hundreds of people, not one has said the information was memorable. Participants have mentioned CFO's giving financial talks, doctors giving medical presentations to colleagues, highly specific, sometimes scientific material. Somehow the speakers people remember manage to move their presentations out of the realm of pure information and make them memorable. In this exercise, quite often people start by saying "I don't remember a lot about the details of what was said, but,…", and then they invariably talk about the story, the humor, how it related to the audience, as well as many other things, but never, never, never is it about the information. Hmmm? Isn't it ironic than that when it's our turn to speak, we create information laden, dull, and technical material.

I'm not suggesting that you not include any information in your presentation. Details, data and facts in the proper context will lead to insight and help to build your case. What I am suggesting is that too much of a good thing will not be remembered and even more importantly will get in the way of the key points you want your audience to remember. What's the alternative? Let's look at that now.

Spice It Up

I like to think of creating content for presentations in terms of cooking. If we were making a soup or stew, we'd start with some basic ingredients: water, meat, potatoes, carrots, and onions. After we cook these ingredients, we would have a meal, it would prevent starvation, but it would be pretty bland. In order to enhance the flavors of the vegetables and meat, we would add some herbs   and spices. Content ideas are like spices. They bring out the flavor of the presentation, making it satisfying and more memorable.

Just as in our spice cabinet, there are lots of possibilities to choose from. Let's take a look at them now.

Chapter 11 Exercise

Identify a time when you were an audience member and witnessed a really great speaker. What was it about that speaker that made them memorable? List the characteristics or what they did that made them stand out from other speakers.

Speaker's Name	Memorable Characteristics/Actions

Chapter 12
PERSONAL EXPERIENCE

My personal favorite content idea is the personal story. I believe this is the strongest feature you can add to your presentation to bring it to life and create connection with your audience. Using your personal experiences is powerful for a several reasons. They are easy to remember. After all, they happened to you. It's your experience. While this does not require much from your memory, it still requires focused reflection to recall key points that make the story relevant to the talk you're giving. It will also take practice to effectively deliver only the relevant points and not all the nonessentials. Another reason personal stories are so effective is that they open the door for greater connection with your audience. They give the audience more to relate to about you as a person. Memorable speakers who are consistently rated among the best share their personal experiences.

WARNING!

If you share your personal experiences by rote, without being in touch with the experience itself, they will not have the same power. In fact, they will feel hollow. This is one of the complaints I have about many professional speakers. They share powerful personal episodes, yet the telling of it hundreds of times has left the occurrence devoid of emotion and meaning. If you choose to add this spice to your soup, make sure it's fresh or it won't add the flavor you desire.

WARNING #2

Make sure the experience you're sharing is relevant to your audience and the point you want to make. We've all heard speakers who tell their entire life story, and felt like we were caving in from too much information. This type of "sharing" is really the ego gone wild. Remember the purpose of your presentation. Share what is of value to your audience. It's all about them. They are sitting there listening for how it's relevant to them.

Chapter 12 Exercise

Right now, write down any personal experiences that have
shaped your belief system, values, or have been significant in
some way. Don't eliminate them yet, just because you don't
think they are relevant. You're just mining your experiences to
create a library of future material.

1._____
_____

2._____
_____

3._____
_____

4._____
_____

5._____
_____

6._____
_____

7._____
_____

8._____
_____

9._____
_____

10._____
_____

CHAPTER 13

Stories

Stories about other people and events are another way to bring your presentation to life. As with personal stories, we in the audience like to see our commonality with others. It's reassuring to know that we are not alone, that others have had experiences like ours. It's good to hear about circumstances that others have faced that we can learn from or be inspired by. We like stories. We have since we were little kids, getting mom or dad to read to us before bed. It's one of the reasons people like the movies. Stories help us make sense out of complexity in our lives.

I have had the good fortune to come from a family of story tellers. I got some insight into the reason once when Chuck and I were visiting two of my aunts and their husbands in Arizona. Chuck commented that he was amazed that my family members can spend the whole day entertaining themselves just talking. My Aunt Vera shed some light on the reason why. "We all grew up on a farm and had to work in the fields. There weren't Walkmans or I Pods, or any of the electronic devices we have today. We had each other, so we talked, told stories and jokes." In my family, not being able to tell stories or at least be a good conversationalist is grounds for disownment. Well not really, but you get the picture.

To this day, I love stories. I even collect them. I keep them in a library of material for speeches and workshops. I catalog them according to topic. One of my favorites is about teamwork. It was sent to me by one of my other aunts (I have a big family!) who has discovered the power of the internet and email. Frequently, she sends me quotes, stories, chain letters and miscellaneous jokes to lighten my day. On occasion, one of these tidbits makes into my content library. This story was emailed to me by my Aunt Doris and is about Charles Plumb.

Charles Plumb was a U.S Navy pilot during the Viet Nam War. When his plane was shot down, he parachuted into enemy hands, was captured and spent 6 years in a North Vietnamese prison. He survived this ordeal and has written a book, "I'm No Hero", about his experience. He also gives inspirational speeches about the lessons he learned.

One day while he was sitting in a restaurant, a man at another table came over to him and said, "Hey, you're Plumb! You flew jet fighters in Vietnam from the aircraft carrier Kitty Hawk. You were shot down!"
"How in the world did you know that?" asked Plumb
"I packed your parachute," the man replied. "I guess it worked!"
Plumb assured him, "It sure did. If your chute hadn't opened, I wouldn't be here today."

That night, Plumb couldn't sleep. He kept thinking about the man. Plumb says, "I kept wondering what he might have looked like in a Navy uniform. I wondered how many times I might have seen him and not even said good morning, how are you?' or anything because, you see, I was a fighter pilot and he was just a sailor."

Plumb thought of the many hours the sailor had spent at a long wooden table in the bowels of the ship, carefully weaving the shrouds and folding the silks of each chute, holding in his hands each time the fate of someone he didn't know.

Now Plumb asks his audiences, "Who's packing your parachute?" Everyone has someone who provides what they need to make it through the day.

I find this to be a powerful story that demonstrates the importance of every member of a team, not just the stars or the most visible.

Using a story like this or a personal experience at the beginning of your presentation it a great way to immediately engage your audience. Remember the purpose of the Open is to engage. Using content ideas immediately in your Open is a great way to grab your audience from the start.

If you can't think of any relevant stories to include in your presentation now, start listening for them today. That's how I started. I began by paying attention, writing them down, and then organizing them so I could access content as I need it if my memory fails me when creating a speech. As you continue to collect and build your content library, you'll be surprised how quickly it grows, and how often others make contributions. Also everything is fair game for me. If I see something in a movie, witness a real life drama at the grocery store, hear it in a speech, or someone else tells it to me in a conversation, I include it in my repertoire, just as I would in a conversation. For example, I've coached people who tell me they don't come across good material. That only happens to other people, like me for instance. At that time, I may describe one of my favorite scenes from a movie called Dumb and Dumber. Many of you may not have seen this movie because it was written with 12 year old boys in mind. I have my son Alex to thank for this one. There are a couple of scenes that are brilliant, (and several I can pass on.). One of my favorite scenes is at the very end, when Harry and Lloyd have lost everything after traveling across the country. They're standing on the side of a road hitchhiking home to New Jersey from Colorado, lamenting their bad luck when a bus pulls up next to them. On the bus are several bikini-clad beautiful young women heading to a sun tanning contest. Leaning out of the door of the bus, they ask Harry and Lloyd "Do you know where we can find a couple guys to apply suntan lotion on us at the tanning contest?" Watching this in the theatre for the first time I was thinking, great, their luck has finally changed. But no. Lloyd scratches his head, pauses and says, "I don't know anyone, but there is a town just down the road. You might be able to find someone there." Everyone in the audience reacted with a sigh, as once again, they prove they really are the dumbest guys on the planet. Suddenly, Lloyd gets a look on his face like he has realized his stupidity and he shouts for the bus to stop. The girls look out the windows and open the door. We're sure he's recognized the error in his judgment. But instead he says, 'I'm sorry, the town is that way,' pointing in the opposite direction. You think the scene is over but Harry turns to Lloyd and say "Boy those are going to be some really lucky guys. Why doesn't anything like that happen to us?'

That story gets filed away for use when someone is lamenting their perceived lack of opportunity or good fortune. It always gets a laugh and really brings the point home.

Recently I had the good fortune of seeing Scott Adams, the creator of the Dilbert cartoon, speak at conference where I was also speaking. He shared his personal experiences. It was very funny hearing about his path to becoming a cartoonist. The thing that stayed with me though, and has given me some real inspiration, was a very short anecdote. He told how at one time he listed all the good things that happen to him and put them into two columns. One column was for successes he had planned for and one for the ones that had been unplanned. He then said that the list of the unplanned successes was much longer than the planned. I use that story as inspiration for myself and clients when it looks like things are not going the way we want.

Today my library is really just a notebook, but it's growing fast. Most of the content I know like old friends, and occasionally I review it to get reacquainted with something I may have forgotten. I think as long as the retired family members are using the Internet, I'm safe from running out of new material.

Chapter 13 Exercise

List any stories you've heard that have captured you're attention.
Do it right now. Don't wait! You have some that are part of
your regular repertoire. Be sure to include those.

1._____
_____

2._____
_____

3._____
_____

4._____
_____

5._____
_____

6._____
_____

7._____
_____

8._____
_____

9._____
_____

10._____
_____

CHAPTER 14
Other Ingredients

Imagery

The art of using language to create a mental picture is quickly being lost. In our rush to get information deployed, we miss the skill of eloquence. Using imagery enables you the speaker to create an environment for your audience, to have them "be there" with you, experience what you experienced. Once again, this requires practice. Writing is a good exercise to develop the ability to see the specifics and describe them. One of my favorite examples of the use of imagery is the description of the late actor Peter O'Toole's eyes. In describing them, you could say were blue or even baby blue. However a description I heard creates a more vivid, memorable picture: O'Toole's eyes looked like they had swallowed a blue moon and they sparkled.

My husband Chuck and I were discussing the purchase of a new car and he mentioned he had seen the new Volvo SUVs and thought they were pretty nice. Our son, Carter, moaned while rolling his eyes, saying we couldn't get a Volvo because, "they're so socks and sandals." I immediately had a picture in my mind of how he perceived Volvo owners. Not just what the people who owned them wore on their feet, but their character, politics and the kind of food they eat.

Using imagery effectively takes reflection, getting into the details, and describing specifics. Is the box red or is it fire engine red? Is it fire engine red or a Chinese lacquer red with a shine so polished you can see your reflection. Not only will the use of imagery engage your audience, it will put you in closer touch with the emotion of your experience.

Metaphor

The purpose of using a metaphor is to bring understanding to something complex or sophisticated. As a byproduct, they are also engaging and interesting.

When you are presenting, you are communicating ideas, concepts and thoughts that may not be familiar or fully understood by our audiences. Metaphors are a means by which you can take something familiar or part of a common experience and compare it to explain, make clear or embellish something you're talking about.

I used the metaphor of cooking to explain how to use content ideas to enrich your presentation. A metaphor I hear frequently is "It's like herding cats" to describe getting groups to focus.

Here's another one of my favorites. "We are all dancers in the ballroom of life. Some of us are accomplished dancers. Some of us can't find the beat."

Contrast

Like the metaphor, contrast brings understanding to the complex by comparing opposites. A client who is in real estate development described the cyclical nature of his business by contrasting different regions based on where they are in their cycle of birth, growth, maturity, decline, and death.

Another client descried his father's garage, using vivid imagery, contrasting the cost of the objects in the garage (car, tools, radio, and calculator) with their costs today.

Political candidates almost always use this technique in their campaign speeches, to illustrate, compare, and characterize their positions versus those of their opponents.

It's the comparing that guides insights. We do price comparisons, historical comparisons, points of view, objects. All this contrast is designed to influence the audience to our viewpoint.

Humor

Humor is the elixir of life. This content idea is at the top of ideas to make our content memorable. This may throw some into a state of panic. "Oh no! I'm not funny. I can't tell a joke." Using humor in a presentation is more extensive than joke telling. In fact, whoever told speakers to start their presentations with a joke should be drawn and quartered. Just kidding!

The first rule of humor in a presentation is that it must be relevant to the audience and the topic. That's one of the problems with those ice breaker jokes. Besides being bad, they don't have anything to do with the presentation or the audience. So relevance is number one. The second rule is to resist anything disparaging. Using humor that insults is inappropriate and detracts from the presentation.

Other than that, tickle our funny bones, make us laugh, amuse us. As audience members, we like the relief of humor, especially in dry or technical presentations. For those who don't feel like you're funny, think of it as being light hearted. The main point about humor is taking the heaviosity out of our presentations.

I work with many professionals in financial services. I will hear often that humor is inappropriate because, "after all, we're talking about money. Nothing is more serious than money!" I say 'Lighten up!' 'Give us a break.' You can be light hearted, even humorous, and be serious minded. Think about it for yourself. Who would you rather listen to, someone who can engage and amuse you or someone who only communicates in a dead serious manner? Dead serious 100% of the time loses its credibility and becomes tedious.

I've heard inappropriate humor, but I have yet to find a situation when humor wasn't appropriate. A couple years ago my grandfather died at the age of 98. At his funeral, a man in his early 70s spoke. He had worked as an adolescent on my grandfather's farm. He told the story of Grandpa calling him over and saying he had a question. My grandfather then asked, "Tom, do you know the difference between a cow's tail and a pump handle?" Tom said he was nervous about giving the wrong answer, so he answered, "NO". My grandfather replied, "Well, I guess we won't be sending you for water!" Ba dum bum.

Everyone laughed. Instantly we were all connected to the joyful memories of Grandpa at a time when we might have only focused on our sadness and loss. Even at times of grief and difficulty, humor can raise us up and lighten our spirit.

Name Dropping

We live in a People magazine world, where fame, infamy, and celebrity get our attention. Using name dropping is a way to get your audience to perk up their ears and pay attention. When I talk about name dropping, it's not just the rich and famous from the entertainment world. It includes business leaders, political figures, and even people in your own organizations, associations, communities, and neighborhoods. It encompasses anyone, any name that is meaningful to your audience and will cause them to sit up and listen.

Personal testimonials are also in this category. If it comes from someone everyone knows who has a relevant reputation, this is name dropping of the highest order. Comments from like minded individuals the audience can relate to or would like to know lend great credibility.

Weird and Wild

Not only do we live in a People magazine society, we also live in a National Inquirer world. Admit it! You look at the headlines or flip through the pages while waiting in line at the grocery store! Our attention is drawn to things that fall outside the norm of our lives. I'm not just talking about things like 100 year old woman gives birth to alien baby with dog head. I'm talking about the less bizarre things that are outside our typical experience. This could include exotic locations, unusual foods, eccentric people or activities. Remember, these are things that would be unusual from your audience's point of view, not yours.

When my children were younger, we had a nanny, Rose. Rose was from the Atlantic region of Canada and was unaccustomed to some of the things that for our family were normal. On one occasion, I left a note asking her to prepare couscous as part of dinner for the kids. She called me at work, sheepishly asking, 'Teresa, what's couscous?' It definitely fell in the weird and wild category for her.

Benefits

This content idea is actually a theme that should be woven throughout your presentation. Benefits answer the questions 'What's in it for me?' and 'Why do I care?' This is of critical importance in business when you want to say specifically what customers get out of your product or service. Don't confuse the features of your product or service with the benefits to the customer. It may have dual processors, but it's the speed and performance of that feature that every customer wants to do more work, better and faster. If you know and understand your audience, this one should not be difficult at all. In fact, you probably have already addressed this if you did Power to Connect in preparation of your presentation. If you find you have difficulty, get back to basics and talk to the people you want to support with your service or product. If you did a survey of the people you want to move to take action, what would the three key things they want from a product like yours be? In fact, why not do a survey? It would be a very credible source to refer to in you presentation.

Current Events

Because of their immediacy and topical nature, current events capture our attention. Current events appeal to our sense of curiosity just like Name Dropping and Weird and the Wild. Millions of people everyday read newspapers, watch the news, and increasingly stay current using the internet. All this is in attempt to stay up to date in a rapidly changing world. When you mention any of the current events affecting your audience's life, it feeds into the need to know and to be part of the flow driving many people.

Facts and Statistics

Facts and statistics are a great way to add credibility and substance to a presentation. When I mention this content idea to CFOs, accountants, financial professionals, their eyes light up, until I add that how they are currently using this idea is putting people to sleep and no one is remembering what they're saying.

There are facts and statistics and then there are facts and statistics. Don't worry. This isn't doublespeak. What I'm referring to are dry, uninterpreted facts and statistics, which include actuarial tables, put in a presentation with the hope that they will make it more interesting.

Like the other content ideas, facts and statistics have to be made relevant, so the audience can understand what the numbers mean. I don't know about you, but I really don't have any idea of how much a billion or a trillion is. I know it's a lot, but I can't really comprehend the magnitude of these numbers. I came across the following statistic that helped me grasp these enormous figures. One in a million is the same as one second out of 11 days. One in a billion is equivalent to one second out of 31 years. Now that I can understand.

I was watching a cable news channel one evening as they were discussing the impact a proposed budgetary item would have on the overall economy. Up to that point, all the commentaries I had heard had thrown about numbers with lots of zeroes behind them. I really wasn't able to understand if the impact was significant. The numbers weren't relevant to me. The expert that day made an effective comparison. He suggested looking at the US economy as the driving distance from Washington DC to Los Angeles. He then said 'If you were to take the economic impact of the budgetary initiative as a percentage of the economy and drive that distance, you wouldn't get outside of the Washington Beltway'. I have some experience driving cross country and some experience driving around Washington. Aside from terrible traffic, the actual mileage is insignificant. That's all I needed to know to make a decision to support or not support the proposal. Even for someone who hasn't done the actual driving, we've all seen the map of the United States or have driven some part of the country so it becomes a more meaningful expression of the facts and statistics.

Think of the use of facts and statistics like USA Today. When the newspaper began, it was ground breaking with its colored masthead and innovative graphics. When talking about revenue at a cosmetic company, the newspaper used lipstick tubes in the bar charts. Population charts were demonstrated with people. I'm suggesting that speakers use the same innovation when it comes to using numbers and facts in their speeches. A good question to ask when including any facts and statistics is 'What does this mean?'

Chapter 14 Exercise

Begin compiling all the content ideas you can think of. Again, don't worry now about when or how you're going to use them. Just get them down. Later as you are preparing for a presentation, you can review what you've collected and check it for relevance. To get you started, you can take some of the ones I've listed in the book.

1._____
_____

2._____
_____

3._____
_____

4._____
_____

5._____
_____

6._____
_____

5._____
_____

8._____
_____

9._____
_____

10._____
_____

The next step in creating a memorable presentation is to take the outline you created in the Structure section of the book, and choose the content ideas that will bring your information to life. Be specific about the elements you use. Don't just write "Share personal experience" Write down which personal experience. If you intend to use a metaphor, write down which metaphor. Write these in the column, Content next to the appropriate section of you presentation.

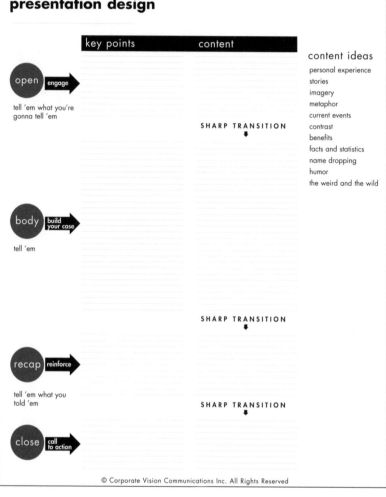

B R A V O
presentation design

key points	content	content ideas
open engage		personal experience
tell 'em what you're gonna tell 'em		stories
		imagery
		metaphor
	SHARP TRANSITION	current events
		contrast
		benefits
		facts and statistics
		name dropping
body build your case		humor
tell 'em		the weird and the wild
	SHARP TRANSITION	
recap reinforce		
tell 'em what you told 'em	SHARP TRANSITION	
close call to action		

CHAPTER 15

Delivery

The most important thing in communication
is to hear what isn't being said.

Peter Drucker

Now that you've created content that will keep our audience on the edge of their seats, the challenge is to deliver it in a manner that keeps them in their seats! Powerful delivery can make or break a presentation. In fact, you can create the best content in the world, but if you fail to deliver it with impact, the content becomes meaningless. Here are the components to a successful delivery.

Windows To The Soul

Let's start with the biggy in delivering powerfully, eye contact. You've all heard the saying 'the eyes are the windows to the soul.' It's true. We humans have an inborn capability of reading one another's inner states through eye contact. Looking into the eyes of your audience establishes relationship and intimacy. It's the way to cross the barrier of "them" and "me" to "us." It gives you both the chance to connect. It's also where you "hear" what they're saying. If you're not paying attention, you're missing their part of the conversation. Your eye contact lets you read all the non-verbal cues your audience is giving.

The face is the only place on our bodies where the muscles connect directly to the skin. This gives us the ability to have a multitude of non verbal signals. Scientist Paul Ekman discovered that facial expressions are the same all over the world, cross cultures. His findings showed that congenitally blind babies will smile at their mothers, having never seen a smile, and that anger, disgust, happiness, fright look the same across the globe. What this tells us is that we have a sophisticated communication system that is broadcasting our inner thoughts to anyone who is paying attention. As a speaker, establishing eye contact with your audience is how to pay attention to the other person in the conversation

Since eye contact requires an openness and vulnerability, many speakers avoid it. Yet the relationship, intimacy really, that is available when your attention is fully on another person is powerful.

Let's give some definition to what eye contact is and what it isn't. Eye contact is looking directly at an individual or group of individuals. It's looking into their eyes and at their face, letting your gaze linger with them. When speaking to groups of 100 or fewer, it's easy to look directly in each individual's eyes. With larger groups, especially in venues with staging and lights, visualization is necessary. Look at sections of the room, including the wings and the back. Linger with each section, letting them see that you are looking at them. The end result is to have each person in the audience feel as though you are speaking directly to them.

What It Its Not

Eye contact is not a fixed stare, boring into the receiver. There is no intimacy there, just intimidation. It also is not what I call "hosing down the audience", with your gaze glancing from side to side, without ever really landing or being present to anyone.

CHAPTER 16

The Power Of The Pause

"It is the space between the notes that makes the music.
Without that emptiness, that silence between,
there's not music, only noise. "

Author Unknown

One of the greatest techniques available to a speaker is, ironically, silence. We view silence as awkward gaps that need to be filled quickly. That silence, the pause, serves many functions. The first is to emphasize a key point. By pausing after a key point or statement, the presenter signals the audience to pay attention to what was said. In effect the speaker is saying, 'This is important. Listen up.' It also gives the audience time to digest the importance of what you're saying.

Secondly, pausing gives the presenter an opportunity to check with the audience to make sure the point registered. By pausing and using eye contact, you can determine if what was said was received or if it needs restating differently.

A third reason to pause is to signal that you have completed one thought or subject and are moving on to something else. These pauses or transitions give audiences a road map so they're never lost in your presentation.

> *"The right word may be effective, but no word was ever as effective as a rightly timed pause".*
>
> —*Mark Twain*

Finally, pausing enables us to find our way back when we've lost our place or forgotten what we planned to say next. This replaces the tendency to ramble our way back on course.

Pausing is one of the most underutilized tools available to speakers. By opening up the silence, audiences will find it easier to grasp the critical points you want to make, and they will have an easier time following what you have to say.

CHAPTER 17

Vocal Texture

Having variety from what is considered to be the norm in pacing, volume, and urgency adds vocal texture and is more interesting than the monotony of staying in a continuous, mid range groove. Think of your speech as a symphony and your voice as the musicians. Each symphony is comprised of several inwardly related movements, with contrasting style and pace. You can have the allegro with its brisk lively pace compared to the adagio with its slow leisurely tempo. Crescendo is the steady increase in volume to reach a dramatic conclusion. Imagine if Beethoven wrote his 5th Symphony in monotone, the repetition of a single pitch. The richness of the famous opening four note motif followed by the gentle lyrical second movement would be lost to us.

Pacing

Most of us speak at a rate that is easy to listen to and follow. Of course there are those whospeaksofastthatitisimpossibleforthebraintounderstandwhatisbeingsaid. At the opposite end of the spectrum are those who s p e a k s o   s l o w l y   y o u   w o u l d l i k e   t o   r e a c h   d o w n   t h e i r   t h r o a t   a n d r i p   t h e i r   w o r d s   o u t. Changing your usual pace adds variety and interest, making you less monotonous. It can communicate your excitement and passion or seriousness and importance.

Volume

Like pacing, we speak in normal tones and volumes that allow us to easily hear what is said. There are also those individuals who speak so softly, that we have to work really hard to hear a word they say or we have to ask the person sitting next to us to repeat what was said. This becomes such an annoyance after a short time that as members of the audience, we finally give up and move on to the thoughts in our own head.

There is a famous management guru (I'm not mentioning names) who screams at his audience through his entire speech. Instead of enhancing the content and making him more interesting to hear, audiences leave feeling exhausted and beaten.

Urgency

Using urgency in your tone tells your audience, this is supremely important. Use it to punctuate significant points in your presentation. Use urgency with caution though. It can be overused and lose its power. One of our clients is a real estate developer and a mountain of a man. He towers over everyone while chomping on an unlit cigar. Several times in his speeches he emphatically tells his audience, this is really important. And he believes it! The problem is that when everything is 'really important', nothing is. It becomes the case of the boy who cried wolf. When something really IS important, the audience doesn't believe you because you've overused urgency.

Chapter 17 Exercise

Breaking Away From The Norm

The best way to find out if your speech patterns are engaging is by listening to yourself speak. Record your own voice. Listen to it carefully several times. Is it pleasant to listen to or does it need some texture? Are the words spoken too quickly, too softly. Is there any variation? If you discover you can use some work in this area, practice byreading children's stories out loud with the intent of keeping a group of 6 year olds on the edge of their seats and paying attention.

CHAPTER 18

Energy And Movement

Energy

It is the job of the speaker to direct the energy of the audience. Each audience has its own personality and corresponding energy level. There is a group I coach that is low key, pragmatic, and very cerebral in their approach to problem solving. Conducting these all day workshops requires my maintaining a high level of energy, increasing interaction between participants to insure the energy doesn't die out at 3:00 with everyone falling asleep. Another workshop is my ADD group. Their energy level is so high, my job is to make sure they don't spin out of control as I'm delivering the material. Individual thinking activities keep their erratic energy focused.

When you are presenting, feel the energy level of the room. There will be times when it will pulse with the collective adrenaline. You as the speaker can harness it and ride it to the conclusion. If you can barely feel the energy, you will have to keep pumping it out until the audience meets your level. It's in these situations that a speaker really earns his keep.

One of the techniques I use to generate energy is to create opportunities for the audience to participate. This can include asking questions, having them talk with one another, as well as activities that require physical movement. As the speaker, delivering with more animation and broader gestures also generates energy.

Movement

In a presentation, there is movement and there is movement (Didn't I say that about Facts and Statistics?). Movement that enhances a presentation and supports accomplishing your goals is what I call motivated movement. The flip side is unmotivated movement, actions that distract, detract, and have no purpose. This includes fidgeting, swaying, pacing, rocking, playing with change in the pocket. Remember that famous management guru who shouts throughout his speeches? He also paces like a caged tiger, leaving the audience focused on his movement rather than the power of his content.

Motivated movement happens for a reason. It supports what's being said and has the speaker connect more with the audience. This is done by establishing a "home" position with feet hip distance apart and soft knees, just like your personal trainer tells you at the gym. From that position, you can easily move in any direction. Always remember to land when you get to where you're going. If you don't, it looks like you are pacing and communicates instability.

WHEN you move is as important as HOW you move. This means moving on transitional phrases rather than walking around the stage. Transitional phrases are the ones between sections in the structure of your content and between the individual points you are making. (Remember sharp transitions?) Never, never, never move when you are making a key point! In theatre, this is called walking on your lines and it's a big no no. When you move while making a statement, attention is drawn to the movement at the expense of focusing on the words. Instead, stand in your 'home' position; make your statement, and then move.

What Do I Do With My Hands?

The question that always comes up in the first day of a Bravo Presentation Coaching session is "What do I do with my hands?" It has a simple and easy answer. Nothing. Your hands know what to do. You don't have to tell them to do anything, just let them go and they will engage naturally and perfectly. Your body is an amazing communication machine. The problem with unnatural use of hands is we try to make them do the right action, which puts us straight in the "doing" realm and removes the authentic action of our communication.

CHAPTER 19

Emotion And Projection

Emotion

A good indignation makes an excellent speech.

Ralph Waldo Emerson

We don't get much support for being emotionally expressive. In fact, when I ask clients to express how they're feeling about their topic, I watch as visions of them making fools of themselves pass before their eyes. We keep ourselves on a close emotional leash, afraid that we'll be seen as out of control, foolish, a crybaby, or over the top. The result is being disconnected from how we feel about our topic.

A client who was president of a large financial services association, as a surprise, planned to acknowledge his son for his professional achievements in a speech to 7,000 members. During rehearsals, each time he began to speak about his pride and love for his son and his accomplishments, he got choked up and fear came into his eyes. He'd say, "Teresa, I don't think I'm going to be able to do this." I encouraged him to express his feelings authentically rather than sanitize and strip them of their emotion. "The audience is going to be touched by this outpouring of fatherly love." As I sat in the audience on the day of the speech and watched as he introduced his son, I heard his voice catch, saw tears come to his eyes. As I looked around,

I saw people throughout the audience, wiping tears from the corners of their eyes too (me included) as we were all touched by his honest show of emotion.

This gentleman could have kept it very "professional" letting only the words say how he felt. If he had, the audience wouldn't have been moved. They would have politely applauded in acknowledgement, but their hearts wouldn't have been touched.

Our speaker could have become incapacitated by his emotions, sobbing uncontrollably and unable to speak, or at least that was his fear. Having your emotions take over in that manner is putting the attention back on yourself and is really an indulgence. Get a hold of yourself and get you're attention back on the audience.

The message here is be in touch with how you feel about your topic, the content or the audience, and express it. If you're excited, be excited. If you're angry, express anger. If there is joy or happiness, make sure you show it. Outrage, shout it out! Don't keep those emotions behind the mask. Communicate them. It's what we'll remember.

Projection

For those who speak to audiences of over 200, projection is critical. I'm not talking about vocal projection, because you will be using a microphone. I'm talking about projecting your attention to the very back row and into all the corners of the room. Much like eye contact for large groups, projection is necessary so everyone in the audience is included. The danger for speakers with larger groups is to concentrate on the first few rows, since they're the easiest to see and interact with. By neglecting the remainder of the room, you will reduce your impact and ultimately your results.

Chapter 19 Exercise

It's now time to give the final touches to the design of your presentation. Look at the structure and content and identify specific delivery directions for key areas of your speech. I don't recommend having each movement memorized. That leads to loss of authentic delivery. You give guidance, what I refer to as director's notes, for high points in the speech, identifying places for dramatic effect, places for special impact.

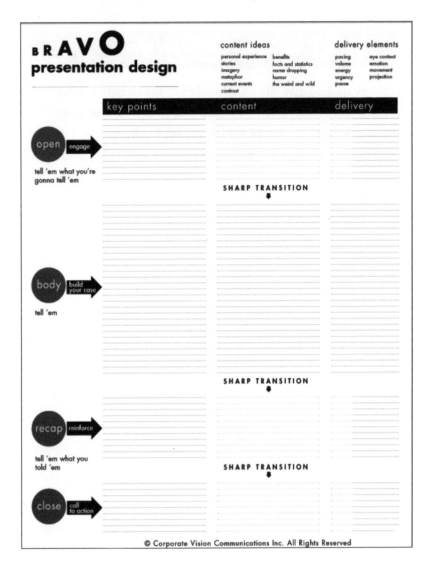

CHAPTER 20

Weasel Words

*Words must be counted among the most
powerful drugs man ever invented.*

Leo Rosten

One way we undermine the strength
of our presentations and our calls to
action is by using "weasel words."
Weasel words are those that let us wiggle out of taking a stand, making a
commitment. They are the words that
qualify, rather than give confidence.

"Try not.
Do or do not.
There is no try."

—Yoda

They take away our leadership. Examples of weasel words are: Try,
hope, want, wish, maybe, kind of, and usually.

Say the following two statements out loud and hear the difference.
"I've tried to show you the reasons why it's important to take responsibility in planning for your future. Hopefully, you've gotten some
value today and will call to make an appointment."

Now read this statement out loud.

"Over the last few minutes, I've outlined the reasons it's important to take responsibility for planning your future. If you've found this of value and would like to explore how we can support you in that process, contact our office in the next two days to schedule an appointment."

Each statement is intended to get the same result, an appointment. One is spoken from a place of confidence, using declarative, committed speaking. The other is spoken from insecurity and uncertainty.

Which presenter would you choose to work with?

Are you moved by the following statements?

- Uncle Sam wouldn't mind if you joined the army
- Don't drink and drive too much
- Do you take this man..? - I'll try

Here are a few more words to watch out for.
But, Ought to, Should, Need to, Can't, Impossible, Doubt, If only, Difficult

Weasel words are words and expressions that undermine your message. They weaken the power of your communication and your commitment to your topic. And...they give your audience room to wiggle out of making decisions and taking action!

CHAPTER 21

Podiums

While I'm at it, let me address one other way speakers undermine their ability to connect with their audience, the podium. In most cases, a podium is a structure that becomes a barrier between the speaker and the audience. For some speakers, it's a security blanket, to hold on to for dear life, to hide behind, to hold notes. None of those purposes supports establishing relationship with the audience. Chuck was coaching a speaker at an event he was producing for the life insurance industry. This speaker insisted on having a podium even after what I thought were very persuasive arguments opposing its use. When the speaker took the stage, he put his notes on the podium, and never looked at them or used the podium. He apparently just needed the security of knowing it was there if he needed it. The unfortunate thing was that this speaker was really good. He was funny, sensitive, animated, had everyone's attention throughout the speech, yet he still felt like he needed something to hold on to, just in case. My advice is – Let go.

CHAPTER 22

How To Practice

"The poem in the head is always perfect"

Stanley Kuntz

Once your presentation is strategized, organized and the content has been created, all that's left to be ready is, you guessed it, practice. It's the part that many speakers avoid, yet it's critical to the success of any presentation. I've heard all the excuses of why it's not possible. All I can say is, if your presentation is important, if the results are meaningful to you, then find the time to practice. Can you imagine Abraham Lincoln giving the Gettysburg Address without practicing it first? Do you think Martin Luther King practiced his "I Have a Dream" speech before he delivered it to the world from the steps of the Lincoln Memorial? In fact can you imagine any leader giving a speech that is intended to move an audience to action without practicing? It seems pretty absurd when you think of it like that. Yet I see and hear speakers all the time who neglect this essential part of making a successful presentation.

So to make it easier to practice, I have a few recommendations. The first is to practice out loud. This is critical. A speech sounds entirely different in your head than it does when you say the words out

> "Everything becomes a little different as soon as it is spoken out loud."
>
> —Hermann Hesse

loud. Some of the phrases you planned to say may not sound as good when you hear them. It's also the only way to hear how some of the delivery ideas, like vocal texture and pauses, sound. There are several ways you can practice out loud. One of my favorites is to talk while I'm walking the dog or driving. After I got over the initial embarrassment of people thinking I was a crazy lady, I found it to be a great time to hear how a speech sounds. The best thing about it is I don't have to carve out more time in an already busy schedule.

For those who have children, reading stories is a perfect place to practice developing more expressiveness in your delivery. Not only do you get to build your skills as a presenter, you make some brownie points as a parent too!

Video taping or voice recording are powerful tools to seeing where improvements are needed. When video taping, if you can assemble an audience, it will make the presentation easier and closer to the real thing. However if that's not possible, I have one client who has his Golden Retriever sit in front of him as he practices.

A journal is a safe place to work out stories, imagery, and feelings before articulating them to others. It's a great place to work out the rawness, the sharp edges, and find the missing pieces.

I have had clients who always write their entire speech out, word for word, then break it down into the outline and use only that for their rehearsal.

Find the practice routine that works best for you so that you go in to any presentation, confident, able to focus entirely on the audience and free to be your authentic self.

CHAPTER 23

Tree Climbing And Other Paths To Authenticity

In the fall of 2002, I surprised myself by publicly stating than my life-time goal is to transform the way people communicate. The way I see myself making that transformation is by teaching and coaching people to focus on the Being and Doing of communication. I must confess though that the Being part of communication is what has really touched my heart and provided me with the greatest growth. Authenticity, Creativity, and Connection. Communication focused on connecting with others, while tapping into and expressing ones true self. And creativity- expressing the right brain capabilities and seeing things through different eyes, being able to see the details in life.

Becoming a communication coach and being on the journey of constantly improving my own skills opens the door to asking important life questions, like what are we afraid of that gets in the way of being authentic? Not being accepted, not being liked, not being appreciated, making a mistake, being laughed at, ridiculed, and thought of as stupid, not being good enough. Yet all that can still happen when we're being someone else, our inauthentic self. What part of ourselves have we walled off, have we let go dormant. My personal experience of deciding I'm not a writer or artist stopped me from doing either of those activities-stopped cold-for 30 years. Making a decision at another time, based on who knows what, someone else's opinion, those voices in our heads, that stop us from   pursuing something we love, something that is a part of ourselves so we begin to live in black and white, bleaching the color of our being from ourselves. What are some of the decisions you've made about who you are?

I decided that at my age, it's not appropriate to climb trees. I didn't even know I had made this decision. I used to love to climb trees. I don't know when I stopped. I probably said to myself only kids climb trees at a time when being seen as a grownup was important to me. And I stopped. Now, if I was incapable of climbing trees, or if I seriously thought I'd hurt myself climbing trees, it would make sense not to do it. But that's not the case. I made a decision that I couldn't do it, and I didn't want to be seen as being a kid. So I climbed a tree. It was a couple summers ago, August, and I was at our family cabin in northern Michigan. I went for a walk with our dog, Maxx, in the fields and woods around the cabin. Maxx is a big, lovable Golden Retriever who doesn't face the same kind of constraints on his doggy self-expression as me or most other people. When he goes into the woods, he knows he's in doggy heaven. He's surrounded by acres and acres of space, animals to chase, smells to experience, and lots of places to explore. The neighboring farmer doesn't appreciate his interest in his cows and more than a few deer have not welcomed him on their trips across our property, but Maxx   doesn't care. He's just a dog who is full out experiencing everything the woods in northern Michigan offer. So Maxx and I went walking in the woods. When I'm in the woods, I usually have some insights about life and myself. On this particular walk, the path curved around a perfect climbing tree. As I was going by it, I noted to myself how perfect it was for climbing. How the branches were just the right distance apart, that they weren't too thick to prevent getting higher and higher. I could see the route all the way up to the top, and not many skinny branches. As I was thinking about how perfect a tree it was and strategizing how I would climb it if I weren't too old, I kept on walking. My thoughts of, 'you're too old to climb trees', 'that's for kids', were competing with a corresponding mental voice saying, 'I'm not too old and besides I'm in good shape. I could climb that tree'. By this time, I was already 50 feet past the tree, on my way to the river. I made a new decision. I made a decision that it's OK for me to climb trees, and I did. I climbed all the way to the top. The feeling of putting my foot on the first branch, of finding a good hand hold, of finding the next branch for my foot and looking up into the branches, finding the best path to the top, was exhilarating. After that initial exhilaration and giddiness, I became concentrated and focused as I chose my way to the top, finding the best way to get as far up as I could. I didn't hear any voices say I couldn't do it. All I could hear was Maxx barking his dismay, like he couldn't believe I was doing this. I broke his image of me too! When I finally reached my destination, I just leaned against the branch and looked around. You know, things look different from the top of the trees and things look different when you don't put yourself in a box too. I smiled at my accomplishment. I have to say it was as satisfying as winning a big contract or anything I've accomplished professionally, because I climbed so much more than a tree. I retrieved a part of myself that day. I returned to myself, my whole self, and I quieted one of the voices that were telling me who I could and couldn't be.

The next day, I went on the same walk with my youngest son, Carter, and my niece and nephew. As we approached the tree, I wanted to tell them I climbed it. I was so proud, but I was afraid to tell them, again the voices causing me to hesitate, then-"You see that tree there? That's a perfect climbing tree" Of course the response was, "How do you know?" "Because I climbed it yesterday", I said with just a little pride in my voice. They responded with a disbelieving, "You did not!" "Yes I did. You want me to show you?" Well, they didn't. They wanted to climb the tree themselves and have me tell them how to do it, without helping. They felt as proud as I had with their accomplishment. What is it about trees that fill us with such a deep sense of connection to something bigger than ourselves?

This is a long way of saying; we've made decisions in our lives that have caused us to seal off parts of ourselves, authentic parts of ourselves, so we don't express them. It shows up in our communication, how we hold our bodies, its stiffness, our unwillingness to use the full range of our voices, our fear of doing something that's not "me". I know that when we reconnect with that, when we unleash that, several things happen. We discover more of who we are authentically. We tap into our creativity, and we're more engaging, more connected to those with whom we're communicating. Those are the kind of people we like to hear speak. This is what will make us better speakers.

How To Reach Us

If you would like more information about Bravo Presentation Coaching, Power to Connect or other products/services we have developed, please visit our website at www.cvcomm.com, email us at info@cvcomm.com or call us 416-696-2020.

We would be happy to provide information on:

- How to order Power to Connect and Presentation Design worksheets
- Our free email newsletter
- How to attend a Power to Connect or Bravo workshop
- Ask the Coach teleseminars (Live and monthly with Teresa Easler)
- How to hire Teresa Easler to speak at your next event
- Books
- Audiotapes
- How to become licensed to teach Power to Connect workshops
- Information on Teresa's upcoming speaking events

For those of you have shared your stories of success in using the strategies from Bravo and Power to Connect, our sincerest thanks. If this book has made a significant impact on you, your family, friends, colleagues, please let us hear about it. We're actively looking for people who are using these strategies to improve their lives. To share stories, email us at info@cvcomm.com.